Called to Preside

Called to Preside

A Handbook for Laypeople

THERESA COTTER

Wipf & Stock
PUBLISHERS
Eugene, Oregon

Nihil Obstat: Rev. Arthur Espelage, O.F.M.
Rev. Robert L. Hagedorn

Imprimi Potest: Rev. John Bok, O.F.M.
Provincial

Imprimatur: +Most Rev. Carl K. Moeddel, V.G.
Archdiocese of Cincinnati, October 3, 1996

The *nihil obstat* and *imprimatur* are a declaration that a book is considered to be free from doctrinal or moral error. It is not implied that those who have granted the *nihil obstat* and *imprimatur* agree with the contents, opinions or statements expressed.

Wipf and Stock Publishers
199 W 8th Ave, Suite 3
Eugene, OR 97401

Called to Preside
A Handbook for Laypeople
By Cotter, Theresa
Copyright©1997 by Cotter, Theresa
ISBN: 1-59752-325-9
Publication date: 7/29/2005
Previously published by St. Anthony Messenger Press, 1997

Dedicated to the many creative, gifted, generous lovers-of-liturgy who
taught me,
mentored me,
inspired me,
worshiped with me,
prayed for me,
told me their stories
and presented me with the opportunities that resulted in this book.

Among them are:

Mary Bednarowski
Lisa Biedenbach
Cindy Moran Boggs
John F. Brandes
John Brooks-Leonard
Philip Brunelle
John Buscemi
Kathy Callaghan
Steve Callaghan
Nansi Carroll
Helen Chambers
Steve Chambers
Anne Vesel Cotter
Benjamin Cotter
Jack Cotter
Paul Cotter
Robert Cotter
Shawn Cotter
Mary Day
Vicky Debbins
Theodore V. Fettig
Anne Cotter Goddard
Steve Goddard
Benjamin Griffin
Toni Grosslein
Dorothy Jean Hensley
Michael Joncas

Mary Staughton Jones
Bob Kasbohm
Donna Kasbohm
Gerald Keefe
Vicki Klima
Josephine Kulbieda
Madeleine L'Engle
Carol Luebering
Ann Magdziarczyk
John Magdziarczyk
Vickie Marr
Madelin Sue Martin
Pat Musenbrock
Clem Nagel
Elizabeth Nagel
Louise Nei
Phyllis Ostrom
Corinne Prindle
Milly Shamo
Edward Soetje
Marilyn Wegscheider
Miriam Therese Winter
Brian Wren
Art Zannoni
Barbara Zimlich
Theresa Zlotkowski

To them I offer my deep gratitude, along with apologies for any errors or
omissions; I remain a student—and lover—of liturgy.

Contents

Introduction

Welcome! With enthusiasm I greet you, presider-to-be! I hold you in awe for you have been called by the Spirit and by your faith community. I offer you this handbook, written out of my passionate love of liturgy as well as my daily experience as church musician, liturgist, lay preacher, lay presider and a member of the assembly.

You have a right to know my stance as I address the topics in this book, so I present them here:

- I believe in good liturgy—meaningful liturgy in which everyone participates;
- I believe in the power of symbols, of rituals and stories, of music, dance and art;
- I believe we are made in the image and likeness of God and that the Holy Spirit dwells within each of us;
- I believe that God bestows gifts to individuals for the benefit of the community;
- I believe in the vision of the Second Vatican Council;
- I believe we, the people, are the Church.

I also believe that good liturgy doesn't just happen. The layperson called to the presiding ministry needs both background and practice to preside well. This book offers information on liturgy and numerous suggestions for practicing presiding skills. You can read through it rapidly for an overview of presiding, but understanding the implications and applications of the material will take time. This book can also be used as a reference throughout your presiding ministry.

The **logo** that appears throughout the book illustrates the approach to presiding offered here.

Presiding begins with **prayer**. The foundation of presiding is the prayer life of the presider. The first three chapters offer reflections on the presider as a person. We will also explore common terms that have special meanings in the context of liturgy.

Preparation begins with the presider's lifetime experiences, coupled with the study of public prayer. Chapter Four deals with the essential matter of symbols, while Chapter Five considers the various elements of liturgy.

Practice is necessary in the attainment of any skill, including presiding. Chapters Six, Seven and Eight suggest methods to sharpen these skills.

In Chapter Nine we come back to **prayer**, the public prayer of the faith community. The prayers that begin each chapter also encourage us to pray our way through this learning endeavor.

Finally, Chapter Ten addresses ways the new presider can meet ongoing presiding challenges through continued growth and learning.

This is an introductory book; topics I cover in a few sentences are themselves subjects of entire books, for a library could be filled with the words written about liturgy, worship and prayer. The resource section at the end of the book suggests places to look for further information.

Throughout the book I use quotations from the documents of the

Second Vatican Council and subsequent Church documents, as well as the official rites books of the Catholic Church. These references establish the guidelines for presiding and for liturgy. The many stories address practical aspects of liturgy and faith.

Since presiding is a public activity, it is difficult for an individual to learn in private how to preside. Group learning is an excellent process for the presider-to-be. The people in the group need only to be interested in good liturgy; the sum of insight and experience is enriched, however, if those who participate are involved in other public prayer ministries. The questions under the heading "Consider" can stimulate discussion within such a group, encouraging you to apply general principles to your local situation.

Because of my love of liturgy, I hope that this book will help you experience what liturgy can be at its best. Finally, I conclude this Introduction with a prayer:

> May the Holy Spirit,
> who is our life and our breath,
> who gathers us to prayer
> and unites us in worship,
> inspire, direct and sustain us,
> for we are all called to ministry in liturgy.
> Amen.

The Call

What is lay presiding? How do we respond to the call to become a lay presider? What do we have to know, to do, to be, to preside?

Spirit Most Holy,
you call us all to be your people,
to love and serve you,
to love and serve each other.
Enflame us with courage and passion
and a new vision of Church!
Grant us wisdom and honesty
that we may respond with faithful generosity
to your call to minister in liturgy.
Direct our decisions;
sustain and excite our endeavors.
We ask this in the name of the Creator,
who blessed us with our being,
and our Lord Jesus Christ,
who graced us with priesthood through Baptism.
You are one God, for ever and ever. Amen.

The Call to Preside

We are called!

As Christians we are called to preach the gospel, to praise our God and to love one another. By our baptism we have both the privilege and the responsibility to minister according to our talents and charisms; all gifts are given for the good of the whole faith community.

Our call to preside emerges from our belonging to a praying community. We are filled with a profound awe at being called to lead the assembly in public prayer; this call is indeed an honor, but a tremendous responsibility as well.

In the early Church when people gathered they chose a presider from their midst. The Second Vatican Council especially recognized the various talents and ministries of the laity. These two traditions come together in our call to be presiders.

Here, at the beginning of the third millennium of Christianity, lay presiders are everywhere! We-who-are-the-Church responded to the Holy Spirit's call to ministry and now serve our faith communities in church buildings great and small, parish chapels, classrooms, funeral homes and cemetery worship spaces, hospital and hospice settings, businesses and homes, senior citizen facilities, retreat centers, prisons and halfway houses, picnic or camping sites—in all manner of worship spaces. By our presence and by our ministry we affirm that any gathering of Christians is the Church.

Laypeople now preside for Morning and Evening Prayer; Word-Communion services; funerals, vigils, committal or burial rituals; Christian initiation rites; school worship liturgies; Sunday Celebrations in

CONSIDER

What do you envision when you hear the term *lay presider*? Why?

What special qualities does the presider who comes from the community bring to presiding?

What unique gifts do you bring to presiding?

What could help you to become an effective presider?

What do you expect of this book? What do you expect of others? Of yourself?

Who in your faith community is available to answer your questions about liturgy and presiding?

The Church earnestly desires that all the faithful be led to that full, conscious, and active participation in liturgical celebrations called for by the very nature of the liturgy. Such participation by the Christian people as "a chosen race, a royal priesthood, a holy nation, God's own people" (1 Pt. 2:9; see 2:4-5) is their right and duty by reason of their baptism. (Constitution on the Sacred Liturgy, #14)

the Absence of a Priest; impromptu prayers, services and rituals; services for a variety of organizations; ecumenical services; communal household ceremonies—all manner of creative liturgies.

We are called! That call to preside may come from the assembly, the parish staff or the pastor. Or the call to preside may originate in the whisperings of the Holy Spirit within us. While our response to the call might be a definite and unqualified yes, often it is a hesitant maybe, reflecting our inner doubts and questions: What are the requirements for becoming a presider? What do we have to know, to do, to be, in order to assume this awesome responsibility?

To begin to answer these questions we need to learn about liturgy, about symbols, rituals and rites. We need to learn about presiding and practice its skills. We need to evaluate our own giftedness and remain open to the workings of the Holy Spirit. Above all we need to pray.

This handbook will help in both the discerning process and the learning process. It can enable us to respond with wisdom, courage, generosity, confidence and enthusiasm. If our call to preside is authentic, the Spirit will ignite within us a desire to preside and to preside well. The most tentative maybe will be transformed into an enthusiastic yes.

▶ *"When our much-loved infant son died of SIDS (Sudden Infant Death Syndrome) my wife and I were devastated. Because our pastor was out of town we asked a lay presider who had himself endured the death of a child to conduct the vigil service. The religious education director who had worked with us in the baptismal preparation program for our so-recently-baptized child presided at the funeral service. The support of these friends and our faith community helped us survive."*

One Approach to Presiding

As our logo reminds us, we begin and end with prayer, and the command to pray permeates all that we do.

Prayer represents our starting point. The presider must be, first of all, a person of prayer, someone who prays in private, with family and friends, someone who participates in the public prayer of the community.

The public prayer of the community is rooted in the private prayer of the members. So too the foundation of a presider's public prayer is his or her private prayer. We recognize within ourselves the desire and need for a relationship with the Divine. In our private prayer we admit our limited yet gifted individuality.

We also recognize that we need a communal relationship with God. We pray with others and we participate in public prayer. Together we praise God with our alleluias, we lament our lack of love, we wonder at the mystery of the human and the divine, we affirm our belief in the sustaining power of public prayer, we recognize Christ in ourselves, in those around us, in our sisters and brothers over all the earth.

Preparation encompasses a wide spectrum of personal knowledge and insights. One of the most profound concepts promulgated by the Second Vatican Council is the recognition of the sacredness and sanctity of everyday life. We are formed by everything we encounter in life; our sacramental and spiritual awareness deepens when we discover God everywhere; we can encounter the holy not only through what has been

CONSIDER

Which steps in this approach to presiding do you think will be most difficult for you? Which will be easiest?

Describe the difference between private prayer and communal prayer.

There is a saying: "The devil teaches us to trivialize our own experience." How might this apply to the process of becoming a lay presider?

Who can help you learn to preside? Consider gathering with a small group of people to discuss presiding, critique your practice and support you in this ministry.

called sacred but also through what has, at times, been dismissed as secular.

Long-range preparation includes anything and everything experienced in life; general preparation for the presiding ministry includes any efforts at acquiring background and developing skills. Finally, specific preparation is involved in preparing to preside at a particular liturgy.

Presiding integrates all we know and believe about God and humanity, all we know and believe about prayer, all we've learned and experienced about liturgy and worship. Life has been a preparation for presiding. Now, as we assume the role of presider-to-be, that preparation becomes more focused, and includes becoming an acute observer of liturgy and presiding, becoming a student of the world of liturgy and worship, becoming a student of the specific rites at which we will preside. Just as a presider is ever in need of prayer, so a presider is to be ever-learning.

As presiders-to-be we are already active members of the assembly of believers. We may bring to the presiding role valuable experience in other liturgical ministries. Eucharistic ministers and sacristans are accustomed to moving in the sanctuary space and handling items used in ritual. Lectors proclaim the word of God in Scripture, read in front of the assembly and know how to use the sound system. Cantors proclaim the word of God in song and understand the structure and flow of the liturgy. Preachers study Scripture, proclaim the word of God and address the assembly. Liturgical dancers move gracefully in the worship space as part of the flow of the liturgy. Each of these ministries is a calling unto itself, but its art and skills can assist us in undertaking the role of the presider.

Practice reminds us to go beyond the mental preparations and physically practice presiding. Begin early to practice the gestures, movements, prayers, greetings, readings, singing, rituals. Practice includes becoming familiar with the worship space, the furnishings and the ritual items, the sound system, as well as coordinating the ministries of the assistants and acolytes, the music director and liturgical musicians, the liturgist and whoever else may be involved in the liturgy.

Finally, we return to *Prayer*. Liturgy is the assembly's prayer, so when we are presiding, we are at prayer in the midst of the whole assembly. Communal prayer is not private prayer that happens to be said in public. This is not the time for the presider to be lost in meditation. Rather, the presider needs to be truly present to the liturgy, to the assembly, to God. This is the assembly at prayer—singing, reading, preaching, praying, moving, listening to God and to each other, responding to the Holy Spirit. We have the honor of assisting all this!

▶ *"I believe in the priesthood of all the baptized and so when I was asked to preside I readily agreed. But when I began presiding I felt overwhelmed—I could actually feel the faith and support of the assembly! These are my friends and neighbors! I never expected presiding to be such a profoundly moving and humbling experience."*

PRAYER
PREPARATION
PRACTICE
PRAYER

CONSIDER

Which of the details of liturgy listed here are the easiest to observe and discuss?

Which of those liturgical details are difficult to observe? Why?

Which do you consider most important to the liturgy? Why?

Which are the most important for the presider? Why?

Which are strengths of your worshiping community? Why?

Which are challenges for your worshiping community? Why?

Which presiding tasks do you find the most challenging? Why?

What gifts and experience do you bring to presiding? How can you use them in the service of the liturgy and of the community?

Observation

Presiders-to-be must first become acute observers. Even before we begin to study liturgy, symbols, Scripture, gestures and all the other elements of presiding we learn to focus on details of liturgy that we never noticed before.

The well-planned liturgy, brought to life through the prayerful ministry of gifted and experienced people, is a work of art. It flows, it has integrity, it is beautiful. At such a liturgy our attention is drawn to the Scriptures, the rituals, the music, the rich silence, the prayers of the assembly, the worship of God.

It is often difficult to learn from fine presiding, since the effective and prayerful presider acts with seeming effortlessness. As a result we may, at first, notice only the negative things: the poorly done ritual, the dropped book, the prayer out of order, the mispronunciation. Gradually, however, the many necessary details of liturgy become apparent.

We observe:

- what occurs in the worship space prior to the liturgy;
- the enhancement, colors and lighting of the worship space;
- the placement of the furniture in the worship space;
- who signals when the liturgy is to begin;
- how the liturgy begins;
- the pace of the liturgy (the entrance procession, the movement, the readings, the prayers);
- the place of music in the liturgy;
- roles and functions of each of the ministers (cantor, lector, acolytes and/or assistants, liturgical dancer, eucharistic ministers, ushers, greeters and sacristans);
- the composition of the assembly (are people with handicaps, minorities and visitors welcomed? are children present in the assembly? are children included and recognized?);
- the presence/absence of directions to the assembly (how are cues given to the assembly? to the liturgical ministers?);
- the use of symbols and rituals;
- the books and other items used in the liturgy;
- the worship aid, missalette or program used by the assembly;
- the visuals used by the assembly;
- the use and effectiveness of the sound system;
- the interaction of the presider and the assembly (the presider's eye contact with the assembly, the assembly's participation and responsiveness);
- how the presider assists or gets in the way of the assembly's worship;
- the gestures and movements of the liturgical ministers and the assembly;
- the attire of the liturgical ministers;
- the body-language of the assembly and of all the ministers, especially the presider;
- the lengths of silence between the elements of the liturgy;
- the type, length and effectiveness of preaching;
- the language of liturgical prayer (is it inclusive? how are intercessions worded?);
- what draws the attention of the person in the pew;

- the relevance of what is being said to what is being done;
- the coordination, cohesiveness and integrity of the entire liturgy;
- what unifies the assembly and liturgical ministers;
- what assists the assembly in its public prayer;
- what distracts the assembly from its public prayer;
- how the assembly concludes the liturgy;
- what the assembly and ministers do following the liturgy.

What a detailed list! With time and practice we develop an acute sense of observation and absorb the feel and meaning of liturgy and presiding. Good liturgy and effective presiding require this attention to detail. Fortunately we undertake this ministry of service to our faith community with the guidance of the Holy Spirit.

▶ *"There's a lot of similarity between being a team athlete and being a presider. The really great athletes always seem to do their job effortlessly and gracefully, which is the result of all their preparation and practice behind the scenes. While they occasionally may be called upon to make a spectacular catch or pass or shot, they usually work at avoiding such spectacular—and risky—maneuvers. Instead, they quietly do their job, are cooperative team members and put the good of the game and the team above their own desires. Maybe more of them should try presiding!"*

Common Words, Special Meanings

The years since the Second Vatican Council have seen tremendous changes in Catholic worship. The reforms were made not because God was ignoring our worship, but because many of us were ignoring our worship. We no longer believed what we were saying and we weren't saying what we do believe. God does not need our worship—we do!

We begin our study of worship with some terms that are common to our everyday language, but have specific meanings when used in discussing worship: *community, assembly, liturgy, celebration, gather, preside.*

> *Holy and beloved Trinity,*
> *first of all communities,*
> *you created us as social beings*
> *that we too may enjoy community.*
> *We are ever yours:*
> *unless you call us,*
> *we cannot gather;*
> *unless you are with us,*
> *we dare not pray.*
> *Excite us in your praise!*
> *Empower us in our worship!*
> *Make us one in loving you,*
> *so that, filled with your presence and grace,*
> *we may love and serve each other.*
> *Grant this in the name of God-made-one-of-us,*
> *who lives and reigns in the community of the Trinity,*
> *one God, for ever and ever. Amen.*

CONSIDER

How do you define community?

Where do you experience community? With whom? Why?

What prevents people from experiencing community?

How can you help bring about community among those around you?

How do you see the role of the ordained presider in community?

How do you see the role of the lay presider in community?

Community

What does *community* mean? Perhaps it is best to begin with what community does not mean. Community does not mean uniformity of thinking, conformity of belief, an abundance of sentimentality, an absence of dissent, a similarity of individuals.

Gathering in community means that conservative stands next to liberal; blacks, yellows, whites, reds and mixed are united in gesture; women and men, young and elderly sing together; Hispanics and Americans of European descent, Asians and Native Americans, are united in prayer to our common Creator; those who come in wheelchairs or are hearing-impaired, those who are mentally handicapped or without sight and those whose anxieties allow them only inside the doorway, all come to worship together.

When we gather in community we are the cosmos in miniature; we are the Family of God. Community means unity with diversity. We are united in prayer, rituals and gestures; we are united in music and in silence; we are united in our common humanity that is both sinful and blessed; we are united in our brokenness and our lack of love; we are united in our mutual giftedness; we are united in our need for love and our dependence upon God.

In community, all are welcomed for all are needed. In spite of our diversity and unresolved discord, we proclaim our unity as though it were perfect! We acknowledge our variance and reconcile it with mutual respect. Our act of faith proclaims that we are ever practicing and straining for the reign of God.

Thus it is that in community:

- we gather in Christ's name;
- we recognize and honor the Christ within one another;
- we respond to the gospel challenge;
- we seek out those in need;
- we work for inclusivity;
- we care for one another;
- we admit our poverty of love and our sinfulness;
- we use our talents and gifts;
- we welcome the outcasts;
- we respond to the call of the Holy Spirit;
- we are the Body of Christ on earth.

In community, through Christ and with the Holy Spirit, we praise our God, Creator of all. In community we do liturgy. When we gather in community we bring Christ's inclusive love, acceptance and healing with us. Through our communal words and actions we bring the spirit of Christ and his gospel to those around us.

Each of us, as baptized Christians, carry Christ within us. It may be the suffering Christ or the infant Christ; the sleeping Christ or the believing Christ; the laughing Christ or the teaching Christ; the tempted Christ or the praying Christ; the crucified Christ or even the entombed Christ awaiting resurrection.

This community in Christ chooses and empowers the presider as its appointed representative. The community recognizes the priesthood of all believers and expresses faith in its own experience. The community tells us what it means to be Church by acting out Church.

▶ *"We sisters had gathered at the motherhouse for a five-day retreat, which turned out to be intensely prayerful and communal. The Holy Spirit was very active! The original plan was to have a closing eucharistic liturgy, but when the priest arrived, we thanked him sincerely and explained that the direction of the retreat had unexpectedly changed. The marvelous spirit of community that had formed throughout those five days of ritual and prayer was too wondrous to be comprehended by a last-minute visitor. We did our own closing liturgy."*

▶ *"I recently attended a friend's funeral, held at the mortuary. The minister who conducted it prayed, read Scripture, spoke, prayed again, read more Scripture, spoke again. A soloist sang two songs. But we were never united in prayer, never united in song, never united in ritual. We never became a community; we all just sat there isolated in our grief."*

▶ *"Whenever I go out of town I enjoy going to other churches for worship. But no matter how good the music, how inspiring the sermon, how uplifting the environment, I miss my community. I realize how much I need my own community for my public prayer."*

Assembly

Before the Second Vatican Council many Catholics spoke of "hearing Mass," as if they were attending a concert. The active role was taken by the priest, who actually needed only one acolyte as "congregation" in order to "say" Mass. In some ways there was less interaction between priest and people than at a play or a concert, where a powerful synergy can occur between the performers and the audience.

The liturgical reform instituted by Vatican II has increased the level of activity in the liturgy. Many of us, as individual members of the assembly, now participate in the liturgy as lectors, cantors, sacristans, greeters, and in other important ministries. The space in which we worship is now unified, with no barrier to keep the people out of the sanctuary, and we likewise recognize a unity of ministry expressed by a multitude of liturgical functions based upon gifts and charisms.

In this new burst of ministerial activity, however, many of us still do not recognize the essential ministry of the assembly. We do not yet understand that we, as members of the assembly, are necessary for a full celebration of the eucharistic liturgy and other liturgies. Most of us do not yet feel the importance of our ministry when we enter the worship space.

Other innovations following the Second Vatican Council, such as the presider facing the assembly and celebrating the liturgy in the vernacular, are minor compared to the implications of the central role of the assembly. When we realize fully the essential role of the assembly we will gain a new understanding of many elements of liturgy. We will understand that roles assigned to lectors, cantors and others are extensions of the assembly's ministry. We will believe that everyone is necessary, that liturgy is diminished whenever any member is not present.

From this understanding of the mutuality at the heart of the liturgy, we will claim our ownership of the liturgy by responsible participation. We will claim the power that is located in the worshiping group because we understand the symbolic sacred function of the assembly. As an assembly we will make a commitment to hospitality. We will demonstrate through our interaction and interdependence, the value of each and every human being, making no distinction according to wealth, prestige or education; age, color or ethnic background; gender, marital status or sexual orientation; physical or mental capability.

Until everyone in the assembly takes ownership of the liturgy, the liturgical reform will be incomplete. Liturgy belongs to the Church—the people—and not to particular ministers. Until we understand this truth and claim our ministry wholeheartedly, we will have difficulty in viewing clearly the role of the lay presider.

Each of us in the assembly, by the "Amen!" of our presence, is necessary to the faith community. The lay presider is chosen by the assembly and has a right and a duty to serve that assembly. By coming forth from the assembly, the lay presider possesses an authenticity within that assembly.

▶ *"I've been a lector since we first had lectors following the council. For a while lectors were seated in the sanctuary during the entire liturgy. I was never comfortable with that, even though I had been an 'altar boy'*

CONSIDER

Do you feel like an essential element of the liturgy when you are *just* a member of the assembly? Why or why not?

How can you be a better member of the assembly?

How can the community be a better assembly?

What is your response to the statement: "The liturgy is lessened by my absence"?

The common priesthood of all the baptized provides impetus for the Catholic people of God to gather in solemn assembly for worship on the Lord's day, normally with the celebration of the Eucharist. (Gathered in Steadfast Faith, #6)

for many years. But lectoring is different from serving! Finally we changed our ritual and now it seems right that I come from the assembly to read and then return to the assembly when I'm done. I am a proud member of the assembly."

Liturgy

CONSIDER

How would you define *liturgy*? What is your experience of liturgy?

What makes *good* liturgy for you?

How important is the role of the assembly for *good* liturgy? How important is the role of the presider?

In the listing of what we do when we gather for liturgy what do you *feel* is the most important? The least important?

In the listing of what we do when we gather for liturgy what do you intellectually consider the most important? The least important?

What is liturgy?

Most of us, if asked that question, would probably answer with something about public worship and the praise of God. Of course, that is what we do when we have liturgy. But the word itself, *liturgy*, means "the work of the people." The public worship of God—liturgy—is the work of the people.

The assembly of baptized believers *does* liturgy. Liturgy is public prayer, communal worship. It is not private prayer done by a collection of individuals at the same time and place, nor is it a performance by a few special ministers. Everyone is to participate. Liturgy expresses our theology while at the same moment it shapes our theology. Everything we say and do in worship is important, not because of God's response, but because of what it communicates to us about what we believe. Every decision we make as a faith community has its foundation in the liturgy.

Gathering for liturgy means:

- celebrating our public memory as the People of God;
- celebrating our faith in the Triune God;
- celebrating our experience of life by telling stories old and new;
- celebrating the times in our life when we encounter God;
- celebrating not only what is but what is to come as though it were already here;
- celebrating our sensuality, our bodiliness, our physical nature;
- moving from a "God and me" relationship to establish together a "God and us" relationship;
- encouraging and supporting one another by the gift of our presence;
- celebrating with song and dance;
- reflecting the radical mutuality that announces the reign of God;
- celebrating forgiveness and reconciliation;
- celebrating, in an atmosphere of love, the priesthood of all the faithful;
- recognizing the worth of each individual;
- celebrating ritual, the familiar pattern of events that is characteristic of all humanity;
- remembering our past and proclaiming our future while being firmly committed to the present;
- celebrating ourselves as the Body of Christ and as the Church;
- being formed, renewed and energized by the liturgy and the Holy Spirit;
- celebrating our baptism and our life in Christ through the Holy Spirit;
- uniting, through our relationship with God, to all others;
- recognizing our lack of love and our resistance to forgiveness;
- celebrating the sacredness and sacramentality of all of life;
- celebrating God and celebrating humanity;

- affirming God's mercy and love;
- celebrating the mystery and gift of life;
- giving thanks to God for our many blessings;
- being renewed in our straining toward the reign of God.

Liturgy is intimately connected with life; it is an icon—a pattern—for living. Composed as it is of symbols, metaphors and rituals it is more real than most other things that fill our life. Liturgy is not only an intellectual experience, but an emotional, physical, spiritual happening.

In every liturgy we celebrate the reign of God—even though it has not yet come fully into being. As far as possible, our liturgy is to reflect the love, justice and mutuality commanded by God since the times of the Hebrew Scriptures.

Liturgy addresses the awesome reality of God and the mystery of our own existence. Through the music, symbol, word, movement and silence of liturgy we hope for insight into the experiences of our life and from that understanding we make connections to our scriptural and faith tradition.

▶ *"I contrast the expectations and understanding of participating in liturgy that we now have with one of my pre-Vatican II experiences of hearing Mass. In my hometown, across the street from a large factory was a church that had a daily noon Mass. At precisely twelve o'clock a priest emerged and began the familiar Latin ritual at a feverish pace. When he got to the offertory, another priest appeared and immediately began distributing communion. They both ended their duties simultaneously and we were out of there, having heard Mass in 13 minutes flat."*

▶ *"When I consider all the changes since the Second Vatican Council, and when I read the Council documents and the commentaries on those documents, I realize that what we really need is a blitz of adult education!"*

Celebration

A word that occurs again and again in our liturgical discussions is *celebration*. We are to *celebrate* our liturgies! Yet, in order to *do* that well we need a better understanding of the term.

Merriam-Webster's *Ninth New Collegiate Dictionary* gives the following definitions of *celebrate*: "(1) to perform (a sacrament or solemn ceremony) publicly and with appropriate rites (e.g., *celebrate* the Mass); (2a) to honor (as a holiday) by solemn ceremonies or by refraining from ordinary business; (2b) to demonstrate satisfaction in (as an anniversary) by festivities or other deviation from routine...."

A celebration marks a day or an occasion with appropriate rites; a celebration is public; a celebration is a change from the ordinary routine.

Nothing in those definitions indicates that a celebration necessarily means we laugh and clap hands and sing and dance joyously—although we may appropriately do all these on occasion. However, we may also celebrate with tears and silence, with keening and heavy hearts. We may celebrate our needy brokenness and our acknowledgement of our lack of love.

CONSIDER

What are your expectations of a celebration?

How would you define or describe a liturgical celebration?

How do you see the role of the presider in a celebration?

How do you see the role of the assembly in a celebration?

How well does your faith community celebrate? How could it be improved?

In a liturgical celebration we respond to our exhilarating and frightening, ecstatic and crazy, awesomely mysterious, God-given life with all of its questions and pains and joys.

An example of a liturgical celebration is a funeral. When we celebrate a funeral it may be:

- a solemn occasion reflecting our wonderment before the mysteries of life and of death;
- an expression of thanksgiving for the life lived;
- a joyous event, as desired by the one who has died;
- a recognition of God's blessing to the community through the life of the deceased person;
- a statement of hope and faith in the Resurrection;
- an experience of searing pain and loss;
- a testimony to life itself—past, present, future;
- an emotionless event;
- a tremendously moving experience.

For those who gather, a funeral celebration may somehow be all of these things at once.

Our liturgical celebrations have many variations. We celebrate feasts for Christmas and Good Friday. We celebrate in major keys as we sing "Alleluia" and "Jesus Christ is Risen Today"; we celebrate in minor keys as we sing "Lord Have Mercy" and "My God, My God, Why Have You Forsaken Me?" We have rituals for both birth and death. We celebrate with awe-filled silence the mystery of being human before the Divine. We celebrate our lived experiences as we tell stories while surrounded by friends and neighbors and friends-to-be. We celebrate anytime we gather to praise God for the miracle of life.

▶ *"One of the most memorable liturgies I ever attended was held in the church parking lot. Three days earlier a tornado had hit the area, causing much devastation, including damage to our church building. We gathered that Sunday morning, as residents of an officially declared disaster area, and greeted one another most anxiously: 'Were you hit?' 'Anyone injured in your family?' Under a sky once again peaceful, we stood throughout the liturgy and praised God, singing unaccompanied and from memory. Through the experience of that tornado, we had been united into a faith-filled and caring community. That day we celebrated life and friendships and community!"*

Gathering

From the liturgical reforms following the Second Vatican Council we have come to recognize the equal importance of the Liturgy of the Word and the Liturgy of the Table. We listen to the proclamation of Scripture and we, as assembly, participate in our own proclamation in the responsorial psalm. As community we consecrate and break bread, partaking of Christ's gift to us.

We have yet to recognize, however, the importance of our gathering for liturgy. Gathering is the basic liturgical symbol, the symbol on which all our other symbols are based. When we, the assembly, gather, we are the Church. With our gathering the Church is at prayer! Gathered as

CONSIDER

What does gathering mean to you?

Why do we not yet recognize the importance of gathering for liturgy?

What significant secular gathering have you attended that has been especially memorable for you? What made it memorable?

How does the recognition of the importance of gathering influence the attitude toward lay presiders?

assembly, we are the Body of Christ! Jesus tells us, "[W]here two or three are gathered in my name, I am there among them" (Matthew 18:20).

Perhaps because gathering is such a natural, human act, we have difficulty recognizing its importance. Perhaps because the simple human act of gathering seems to lack any element of the miraculous we fail to value it as the soul work that it is.

We cannot gather for liturgy unless the Holy Spirit first calls us to gather. And when we do gather for liturgy, we come together in the name of Christ. We gather to pray with and for each other, to respond to the prayers of those who gather with us. By our presence we shout our "Amen!" to the communal worship of God.

When we come together as Christians in response to the call of the Spirit, we gather to:

- lament and weep;
- sanctify time;
- endure silence;
- express grief and gladness;
- shout our rage and to listen soundlessly to God's voice;
- praise the Divine;
- become community;
- ritualize our lives and tell our stories;
- recognize our part in something greater than we;
- express our astonished gratitude for the tragi-comic gift of life.

We gather because uniting is the nature of love! United in our humanity, we come that we might be united with Divinity. We gather to rejoice, but also to acknowledge our need for forgiveness. Recognizing our own brokenness and lack of loving, we gather in need of healing and reconciliation. We gather for comfort, for challenge, for renewal, for refreshment. We gather in longing for the reign of God. Open to God and neighbor we gather to welcome the outcast and recognize the integral unity of the human person. We gather in hope of full union with God through a dialogue between the Divine and our human hearts.

No belief statement is mightier than the declaration we make when we gather! Until we recognize how crucial our gathering is, we will not be able to savor fully the importance of liturgy. Neither shall we be able to value our own role as the assembly, the primary minister of the liturgy. Because of the importance of gathering, the liturgy is lessened by every absence—including our own! Only when we become convinced of the importance of the assembly's gathering will we be able to respond wholeheartedly to the role of the lay presider.

▶ *"I was fortunate in getting to know two priests from Uganda who were studying in the United States. Their preaching was fascinating! They always began their sermons with greetings to the gathered assembly from all those they had met during the previous week. They explained that this was their native tradition; all the people they had visited during the week—the ill and homebound and those in faraway villages—all sent their greetings to the assembly. The Ugandans have such respect for community and for the gathering for liturgy that each one had to be present—if not in person, then in spirit and in greeting."*

PRAYER
PR**E**PARATION
PR**A**CTICE
PRA**Y**ER

CONSIDER

How would you define presiding?

When have you led prayer? Did you consider that presiding? Why or why not?

What do you see as the difference between ordained and lay presiding?

What is your response to the statement: "Good presiding is good presiding, and poor presiding remains poor presiding, no matter who the presider"?

How do you feel about becoming a presider yourself?

What do you see as your greatest challenge in being an effective presider? What can you do to overcome that challenge?

What gifts and talents do you bring to presiding?

Presiding

What is presiding? Beginning with the simplest, broadest definition, "Presiding is enabling others to pray." This definition links together:

- a parent assisting a child at nighttime prayers and a bishop officiating at an ordination;
- the family united in ritual and the camp counselor conducting prayers around the campfire;
- a teenager offering table prayer and a priest saying the Eucharistic Prayer;
- the secretary saying the opening prayer for the noon Bible study group and the monk presiding at Liturgy of the Hours;
- the youths leading the school prayer service and the nun leading her community in prayer;
- the person officiating at a burial site and the person officiating at the Sunday worship;
- the lay pastoral caregiver bringing communion to the bedridden and the preschool religious education teacher leading children in the Sign of the Cross.

We tend to think of presiding as a function performed in formal situations, as in a church before the assembly. Yet all the instances mentioned above are examples of presiding: from cathedral to bedside, from chapel to graveside, from home to school to everywhere! Anytime we lead prayer with others we are presiding and serving as a model to those with us.

For the purposes of the present discussion, however, we add to this definition the recognition of the presider as a representative of the community: "Presiding is serving the faith community by enabling it to pray."

We may see differences in the degree of formality and solemnity or in details determined by the particulars of the situation, but no line separates enabling prayer and presiding.

Nor is there any distinction in the standard of presiding for the ordained and the lay presider; good presiding is good presiding, and poor presiding remains poor presiding, no matter who the presider! As lay presiders we do not worship a lesser God, nor does the assembly who worships with us deserve inferior presiding.

Enabling or empowering the community to pray is most certainly a privilege. It is also a right that we have as baptized members of the community, limited only by our gifts and talents. The presider is a symbol of what the community is called to be: As baptized Christians we are always examples to each other of Christ on earth.

The lay presider can serve the faith community in many ways. With reverence and hospitality guiding our words and actions, we enter into the lives of those around us and empower them in the traditional and familiar rituals and liturgies and in prayer-filled new rituals; we help facilitate the assembly's doing what they are called to do.

From our understanding of the liturgy as the work of the people comes our understanding of the varied roles of ministry, including that of the presider. In all liturgies, our function as presider comes from a call to serve the people.

We who come from the assembly, who are members of that faith community, bring to our ministry an authenticity to that assembly: We have been called.

▶ *"Years ago, when I first became a lay presider, I began my preparation with information about the ministry and I carefully gathered it together in a box I labeled 'Lay Presiding.' A while ago I removed 'Lay' from the title, for I came to the realization that there is no alternate standard of presiding for laypeople; just because I'm not ordained does not mean I have an excuse for doing a poor job!"*

The Art of Presiding

I n much of this book we focus on the skills required for presiding. It is possible, with practice, to achieve a mechanical perfection of these skills. The *art* of presiding, however, transforms rote prayer into prayer of the heart. In this section we will discuss the art of presiding and describe qualities of the ideal presider.

> *Ever-creating God,*
> *Giver of gifts and Source of all good,*
> *we thank you for your gracious kindness.*
> *You have given us a love of liturgy*
> *and a desire to praise you.*
> *Accept us,*
> *accept our offerings of honor and glory.*
> *Liberate us from all that separates us*
> *from you and from each other.*
> *Transform us, that all we say and do*
> *reflect you and your love.*
> *We pray these petitions*
> *in the name of the Creator, Savior and Sanctifier,*
> *one God, who lives and reigns for ever and ever. Amen.*

The Art of Presiding

Effective presiding involves both skill and art. We can learn the skills needed for presiding. New presiders can learn how to move, how to use the sound system, how to read well. New presiders can learn about liturgy and ritual and public worship, environment and vesture and the liturgical year. New presiders can practice singing and preaching and praying aloud.

Without developing the art of presiding, however, presiders cannot move beyond a rote experience of worship. It is the art of presiding that moves prayer from the head to the heart. The art of presiding is not technique; it cannot be taught. The art of presiding, like other forms of art, comes from within us; it comes from our heart, from who we are.

As with our efforts to be a better friend or lover or parent, we can learn techniques to convey more fully what lies within us, but the most important ingredient is love. Learning the various presiding techniques and skills will have limited impact unless we first love what we are learning. We might compare it to building a tremendous vocabulary, but having no thoughts to express.

While we learn how to preside, then, we must nourish a multifaceted love so that we communicate from the deepest part of our being. The art of presiding expresses our love of the liturgy and the worship of God, our respect for Scripture, our recognition of the value of tradition, our willingness to be vulnerable. Through the art of presiding we acknowledge the faith community as the Body of Christ, recognizing the Holy Spirit in each of us. We affirm the importance of the assembly and

CONSIDER

How would you describe the art of presiding?

Who are some presiders you know whose presiding is an act of love? What makes these presiders identifiable?

What are some reasons why presiders may be hesitant or even afraid to regard presiding as an art?

What is your reaction to the idea that presiding is an art? Why?

express our willingness to be truly present to this worship experience. Presiding is an act of love.

▶ *"As the liturgical musician responsible for coordinating liturgies, I'm always concerned whenever we have a visiting presider. However, one elderly priest's whole being exuded the serenity of a life spent responding faithfully to God's call; when he smiled, which was often, he radiated that love. His entire being was enveloped in the art of presiding, so when some specific action or ritual was less than letter-perfect the prayer of the assembly remained undisturbed. At the end of the liturgy, as he was leaving, he gave me a radiant smile. 'I think it was valid,' he said. I nodded confidently."*

The Presider as Minister of Hospitality

CONSIDER

Who and/or what makes you feel welcomed at liturgy? How?

When have you experienced an inhospitable presider? How was that lack of hospitality communicated?

How was hospitality practiced in scriptural times? What were the duties of the host?

How might you be a hospitable presider?

We gather. As Christians, our most basic public action is gathering. In the presence of our sisters and brothers we gather to pray and sing and proclaim the reign of God, to tell the stories of the past and of the present, to hear God's word, to break bread, to give thanks, to confess and to be forgiven, to offer praise, to marry and to bury, to baptize, to bless and to be blessed, to anoint and to be anointed, to comfort and commission.

We gather in hope of encountering the sacred, of experiencing the divine so that we may understand the human, of hearing the answers to the questions we all ask. We gather in faith to be renewed. We gather in the presence of the Risen Christ. We gather in the name of Christ who is within each of us. We gather because our God calls us to community and because the Holy Spirit enables us to gather.

Hospitality is integral to any gathering. In a gathering of Church, hospitality becomes even more important because we gather in response to God's hospitality. Hospitality is the primary function of the presider. Being hospitable is much more than saying "Welcome." Being hospitable means that everything about the presider—clothing, gestures, movements, facial expressions, words and stance—should communicate to those assembled: "Come, let us worship God together!"

The hospitality of the assembly's gathering arises from three sources. Hospitality comes from within the liturgy itself, from within the assembly and from within the presider.

Hospitality is not something added on as an afterthought to a liturgy; neither is it limited to the presider. Hospitality is the work of the assembly, not only during the time of liturgy but throughout each day of the week. An environment of hospitality transforms an empty space into a place where people can gather and be community. Hospitality ensures an environment free of both fear and domination.

At liturgy, the presider expresses the assembly's hospitality, but does not generate it, for hospitality is a quality of the whole community. As minister of hospitality, the presider is both prepared and practiced in the role. The relaxed, flowing liturgy happens because the presider is well-rehearsed and understands what liturgy means. "Winging it," relying on spontaneity, is not being hospitable to the assembly or the other ministers.

Besides preparation and practice, genuine hospitality requires personal involvement, a welcoming of the heart that is but prelude to a sense of community identity and communal engagement in worship. We are enthusiastic, and we do not hesitate to let our enthusiasm show. Even though the occasion may not be joyous, we are genuinely pleased to be privileged to celebrate this liturgy. Somehow, in word and action, we as presiders need to convey to the assembly that of all the places in the world we could be at this instant, here, with this assembly, is where we most want to be.

The presider, as minister of hospitality, is gracious, anticipates and attends to the needs of the assembly, and is relaxed and at ease with the presiding role. The presider knows the assembly and is willing to enter into their lives. The presider is sensitive to and aware of what is happening, while affirming and empowering the other ministers and the assembly as members of the priesthood of the faithful. The presider tries to clear a path for encounters with the Divine—and never stands in the way.

When we preside we become vulnerable in our willingness to be part of something greater than ourselves; we allow the liturgy to happen through us as we become open to the Holy Spirit and to our sisters and brothers in Christ.

Presiding is an act of love; hospitality is an expression of that love.

▶ *"Our pastor truly loves people! That became even more obvious to me when our daughter married. At the wedding rehearsal Father John quickly put all the young people at ease. At the wedding he managed to make the non-Catholics feel a part of the liturgy. For months after the wedding our Protestant friends were still commenting on how welcomed he made them feel!"*

The Presider and Presence

God is always present to us. If God forgot us for an instant we would cease to exist. God's presence challenges our lack of presence. In liturgy we are called to be present to God. The presider is especially called to be present to God, to the assembly, to the liturgy. To *this* place, *this* time, *this* ministry, *this* assembly, *this* liturgy—we are present. Everything about us, as presiders, says "I choose *this*."

To be present, the presider must be vulnerable and accountable. The presider enters into the lives of the assembly—at least for now. A presider who is present to this moment of liturgy is unhurried, takes time for reflection and is open to transformation. The present presider is intentional and purposeful.

To preside is to make a commitment, to be in covenant with the assembly. It is a covenant of trust, whereby the presider assumes responsibility both to the assembly and to the liturgy itself; it is a covenant of presence.

▶ *"Our son Benjamin, who has Down's syndrome, has been a server for eight years. He does a good job—he truly has a sense of presence. What has amazed us have been the affirmations that he has received and the stories that we, his parents, have been told by members of the congregation. Ben's achievements are made known to others who know*

CONSIDER

How important to you is the presence of the presider?

How does an effective presider communicate presence?

When have you sensed a presider was not present to the liturgy? How was this communicated? How did you feel about that liturgy?

What do you think would be your greatest challenge in being present to presiding? How can you work with this?

When are you most present to what you are doing? Why? How might this help you as a presider?

people who are developmentally delayed, but Ben himself has no idea of the power of his example!"

▶ *"When I was hospitalized recently a pastoral minister brought me communion. She was in and out so fast that it took me several minutes to realize what happened. It was not a prayerful event, the pastoral minister wasn't really with me in my pain and there was nothing of the eucharistic experience about it. She might as well have been delivering the mail."*

The Presider as a Person of Prayer

The first and most important requirement for presiding is that we be people of prayer. We pray in private, with family and friends, in groups and in the public prayer of our faith community.

Saying that we are people of prayer is not boasting; we are not saying that we have achieved nearly perfect saintly status. Nor are we saying we have penetrating knowledge or awe-inspiring wisdom. Being people of prayer means that we earnestly seek and work at a relationship with God. It means God is important to us. While the study of Scripture and theology can teach us about God, only through prayer and meditation can we begin to know God.

In our desire for a relationship with the Divine we are not content with a mere rote recitation of prayers; we yearn for more. We seek the God Without—the God of majesty and mystery, Creator of all that is, and we seek the God Within—the Holy Spirit who dwells in each of us, the Christ whose body we are. We listen to God as revealed to us through our experiences, through others, through the Holy Spirit. All this is included when we say we are people of prayer.

In prayer we both hear and respond to the call to preside; in prayer we find the faith and courage, the honesty and humility, the joy and reverence and love, to respond to that call; in prayer we develop the patience with ourselves that we need to follow through in our response.

Prayer, reflection, meditation and silence affect how we preside. They are necessary for our preparation, for our perspective on the ministry and for the wisdom to recognize life-giving, love-engendering, praise-filled words and actions.

Liturgy is not personal, private prayer; liturgy is corporate, public prayer. But when we come to liturgy we bring with us our personal prayer.

CONSIDER

What do you envision when you hear someone described as being a person of prayer? Why?

What are the various ways that you pray? Which is your favorite? Why?

Why is communal prayer important to you?

What is missing when people do not include public and communal prayer in their prayer life?

The Presider as a Lover

We are people of prayer and we are people of love. Without love, taking on the vulnerability of presiding is too risky. Only in love can we allow ourselves to become part of this happening called liturgy that is so much greater than ourselves. And so, we are to be lovers. We enter into our loving, bringing all that we are and all that we have: love of God and of ourselves; love of other people and of community; love of liturgy.

Without love, none of this makes sense. We, limited and finite human beings, offer our flawed, often conditional and wavering praise to our

CONSIDER

What do you envision when you hear someone described as a lover? Why? Do you consider yourself a lover?

What do you feel passionate about in your life? Why?

What does all this have to do with presiding?

Creator—the God of all that is. But over and over again, in Scripture and in our everyday lives, God assures us we are loved. The story of salvation history is the account of God's love for us. That's why we continue to offer our praise and worship; that's why we do liturgy; that's why we respond to God's love with our love.

► *"When I was first asked to become a lay presider I felt unworthy, but then I thought of the absurdity of it all. In liturgy we humans stand before God—the Creator of all that is. What can any of us do or say that is worthy of our God? The astonishing thing is that God has loved us for a long, long time, and shows no sign of tiring of us."*

The Presider as Someone Willing to Be Transformed

We all look to liturgy to be transformed. When people complain about liturgy they often say, "I don't get anything out of it." An appropriate answer is often, "What do you put into it?" But underlying the complaint is the assumption and expectation that liturgy will change us.

The presider is a symbol of what the community is called to be. We are all called to openness, to a willingness to be converted and transformed. We, as presiders, do not do the transforming; as much as anyone else present, we are to be willing to be transformed by the experience of participating in the liturgy.

This is risky. Our openness to transformation makes us vulnerable. We become vulnerable to those around us, to the pain and brokenness of human existence, to the loneliness and longing of the poor in spirit, to the injustices around the world and in our community. This is what participation means.

In spite of the risk we do participate: We listen, we speak and sing, we do ritual, we form community. Sometimes, God's grace appears and we are transformed.

► *"People who don't lector—or do something else equally public—don't realize how much humility it takes to get up there! When I'm a reader I'm making myself vulnerable. I could fall on my face—both literally and figuratively. It would be much easier just to remain in the pew."*

► *"At our communal penance services, we have stations located around the worship space where one or two parishioners do a laying on of hands. This is a stirring way to acknowledge our sinfulness against one another and our need to forgive one another. At a service before Triduum a man with his mentally handicapped daughter ministered at one station. When I stood in front of them, they each put a hand on my shoulder, and, for the first time, I became aware of the suffering my insensitivity to those who are handicapped might have caused. Yet, when they looked at me, I knew I was forgiven. Tears seemed the only fitting response."*

CONSIDER

When have you been transformed at liturgy? When have you felt the Holy Spirit's presence? In what ways do you assist or prevent such occurrences?

In what ways is the statement "I don't get anything out of liturgy" a valid assessment of liturgy? In what ways is it not valid?

How does all this affect presiding?

PRAYER
PREPARATION
PRACTICE
PRAYER

CONSIDER

How do you feel about undertaking a study of liturgy and presiding? Why?

What resources and time do you have for such a study?

Is it possible to be in a group studying liturgy and presiding? Is this feasible for you to do now?

What are some of the advantages of studying liturgy and presiding in a group?

The Presider as Someone Willing to Learn

"God helps those who help themselves." We do not excuse our lack of preparation and practice by saying we rely on the Holy Spirit's guidance. Neither do we content ourselves with old theology, outdated practices or a complacent mindset.

We need to evaluate our willingness to learn, to read and study, to discuss, to practice. The study of liturgy is a lifelong endeavor. A large library could be filled with the words written about liturgy, worship, theology, presiding. Topics covered in two or three sentences here are themselves subjects of entire books and even entire sections of a library.

Along with our willingness to learn is a need to be honest in our evaluation of our abilities. Balancing honesty and humility, we discern how we can best serve the assembly.

▶ *"When I first began presiding for Morning Prayer and Evening Prayer I was so nervous that I could hardly say the words of the liturgy. Eventually, as I became more accustomed to presiding, I realized that the opening greetings for those liturgies are intended to be sung. With some help from our music director I learned how to sing them and now that seems right."*

The Presider as a Believer in Good Presiding

Good, effective presiding is good, effective presiding—no matter who the presider is. And poor presiding is poor presiding—no matter who the presider is. Either the presider enables the assembly to pray or the presider hinders prayer.

Presiders—and anyone discerning a call to preside—must believe firmly in the importance of good presiding. How can we offer God anything but the best? How can we offer our assembly anything but the best? Laypeople who are involved in liturgical ministry must never use their lay status as an excuse for doing a poor job. There is no double standard for presiding. Lay presiding is not a stopgap measure, a temporary solution to a clerical shortage. Lay ministry is ours by virtue of our baptism and in recognition of our individual gifts and charisms. We find historical and biblical precedents for laypeople presiding and preaching. In fact, Jesus himself did not have official status in the established religion.

We who are called to preside have a serious duty to respond with the generosity of time and talent that is needed to do well. We have neither reason nor excuse not to become good and effective presiders. Being called from within the assembly gives us an authenticity that others entering into the faith community have to earn. We who belong to the assembly are most attuned to the needs of that assembly: We know both the brokenness and the glory of this community; we know where love exists and where love is desperately missing. We are authentic to that assembly and we are accountable to that assembly.

CONSIDER

Why would you expect the ordained to be effective presiders?

Why would you expect laypeople to be effective presiders?

Why should there be only one standard for presiding?

What are some reasons you can become an effective presider? What do you have to do to develop your gifts?

CONSIDER

What about presiding makes you the most nervous? Why?

Imagine the worst thing that could happen while you are presiding. How would you respond? How would the assembly respond? How might God respond? How important would that occurrence be in the course of salvation history?

How is pride involved in presiding? How is humility involved?

What talents do you bring to your faith community? How can you use these talents in presiding?

The Nervous Presider

Of course we are nervous. As we approach this new experience of presiding we need to confront this nervousness. Only if we consider liturgy unimportant will we not be nervous. Only if we have no love or respect for the assembly will we not be nervous. Only if we deny the possibility of an encounter with the Divine will we not be nervous. The first thing to remember about nervousness: It testifies to our belief in the value of liturgy and of what we do in liturgy.

Some nervousness is fed by a fear of appearing foolish or doing something wrong in presiding. This can be a matter of pride, which is best remedied with a touch of humility. Responding to the call to preside may mean that we allow ourselves to risk appearing foolish.

The reality of the situation, however, is probably far different from this, for in the liturgy the congregation is almost always on our side. The support of the assembly is a powerful force; the liturgy is their prayer and they, too, want it to go well.

Also, we need to remember that nervousness "ain't all bad!" Professional performers, such as actors and musicians, tell us that no matter how often they perform they continue to experience nervousness. Many assert that not only is some nervous tension desirable, but it will be time to retire or change professions when they no longer experience that nervousness.

This type of nervousness is similar to an athlete's "being up" for an event. This kind of nervous tension brings a heightened awareness that alerts us to what is happening, makes us more sensitive to our task, stimulates us to try a bit harder, helps us focus more intently upon what we are doing, helps us recognize our limitations and opens us to workings of the Holy Spirit. This beneficial type of nervousness helps us be better presiders.

A nervousness that prevents us from being effective, however, is not helpful. This "walking-into-walls" degree of nervousness needs to be avoided. The most effective way to combat paralyzing nervousness is through being both well prepared and well practiced.

Remember our logo. Within prayer we hear the call to preside, discern our presiding gifts and talents and find the courage and humor and self-love to be patient with ourselves. No antidote to nervousness is as effective as being well prepared. Our presiding will go well when it expresses who we are, when we are prepared, when we have practiced and when our presiding is itself prayer.

Of course we are nervous. In the fullness and the poverty of our humanity we dare to come before our God and offer our worship. But we let go of our fear and anxiety; we make our act of faith in the Holy Spirit, who will guide us and be with us. And then we trust in God to say and do the right thing at the proper time. It is in such an atmosphere of love and faith that we do liturgy.

▶ *"Before I preside, I do some stretching exercises and deep beathing, followed by vocal warm-ups like the choir uses. I also practice tongue-twisters like 'Peter Piper picked a peck of pickled peppers.' These exercises help me relax and prepare me for presiding."*

Symbols and Rituals— Building Blocks of Worship

A visitor to our liturgy could learn about our faith by listening to the readings, the preaching, the prayers, the sung texts. But these words of liturgy are outshouted by the beliefs expressed in our actions and symbols. Everything about liturgy is significant; it not only reflects what we believe, but reinforces it. Everything about worship and about God is symbol and metaphor, and everything speaks!

Great Unknowable God,
you are the wind and the silence,
the darkness and the light;
you are simplicity and paradox.
Draw us into your mystery!
Teach us the language of symbol and simile;
sing for us the melody of metaphor.
Unite us in the communion of ritual,
that in our worship
we may be transformed by your love.
We ask this in your name, God-beyond-naming,
who lives and reigns for ever and ever. Amen.

Signs and Symbols

When we gather for worship we are surrounded by symbols, for we are a sacramental church. The importance of symbols in our tradition corroborates our insistence that public worship is not to be just an intellectual experience.

All of us respond to symbols; they affect us emotionally, psychologically, spiritually. To preside well we need to understand this power of symbols and to develop a "feel" for their use in liturgy.

A discussion of symbols usually includes signs because the two categories are interrelated. Also, it is easier to understand the term *symbol* when we contrast it with the term *sign*.

Both signs and symbols are part of our everyday life; we use them constantly in our communication with one another. They can be things, words, movements, music and art, even persons and places. They can include anything we see, taste, smell, say, touch or hear.

Signs convey information; they speak to our minds. Signs label, direct, offer information. A sign usually has only one meaning or possibly a small number of meanings; all other interpretations are wrong.

Language consists of signs. For example, the word *bread*, either written or spoken, is not something we can actually eat, but refers to something edible. Words, numerals, musical notation and mathematical "symbols" are signs. Movements can be signs: a police officer directs traffic with hand signals and whistles; deaf people "speak" to each other using signs. The open door of a business establishment can be a sign that it is open for business. The signs that border our streets and highways

CONSIDER

What does "only a symbol" mean to you?

What are some possessions that you prize only because of their symbolic value? Why? How do others regard them?

What people are symbols to you?

When are you a symbol? Why?

What are some traditions cherished by your family? Why?

What are some holiday symbols that helped form you? What are some holiday symbols that help describe you now?

What symbols do you ascribe to other denominations and faiths? How important are these symbols to those beliefs?

What are some Christian/Catholic symbols that helped form you? Which have you abandoned or discontinued? Which help describe you now?

Respond to the statement: "We are all theologians when it comes to symbols."

announce speed limits, populations, locations; they advertise products or political candidates.

Symbols, especially in liturgical language, are more difficult to define. The word *symbol* has a variety of meanings that can mislead us when we try to define liturgical symbols. For instance, we may say, "It is merely a symbol" when we want to say something is a substitute for what is authentic. Often we use the word *symbol* when we actually mean "sign."

But in a liturgical context the term *symbol* is used in its fullest and most powerful sense. Symbols speak not only to our minds, but to our hearts and emotions. In the presence of symbols we may catch our breath or become tearful or angry; we experience a gut reaction.

Symbols, whether words, objects, ritual actions, persons or places, are based on our experience, not just our knowledge. That is why they speak to the whole person and not just to the mind. In a manner that eludes description, symbols are alive; they point to something beyond themselves. Symbols are larger than life, for they participate in their own reality; they contain within themselves some quality of what they represent. Symbols reveal truths about the meaning of life or patriotism or religion or social mores.

A symbol is a mystery in which we become both identified and involved. Encouraged by the symbol we help the symbol become even more powerful. When we encounter symbols, we are changed. While we have difficulty defining symbols, we know when we have encountered symbols used effectively. After such an encounter, our inadequate account of the experience often concludes with "You just had to be there!"

The following chart shows a comparison of signs and symbols.

SIGNS	SYMBOLS
Have specific meanings	Have a variety of meanings
Are "not alive"	Become "alive" when encountered
Have meanings that are taught or learned	Have meanings known through experience
Are aimed at head-learning	Are aimed at the whole person
Do not extend beyond surface meaning	Refer to universal truths
May be interpreted incorrectly	Cannot be declared right or wrong
Exist independently of people	Exist only when encountered by people

Signs convey identical information to everyone, while symbols can mean totally different things to different people. The meaning of signs can be taught, but the meaning of symbols cannot be adequately explained. Usually we must let symbols speak for themselves.

Signs can become symbols and vice versa. A sign that has touched our experience can be transformed into symbol. For example, to someone

People in love make signs of love, not only to express their love but also to deepen it. Love never expressed dies. Christians' love for Christ and for one another, and Christians' faith in Christ and in one another must be expressed in the signs and symbols of celebration or they will die. (Music in Catholic Worship, # 4)

whose spouse died because a driver ran a stop sign, this simple sign becomes a symbol of shock, pain and loss. It may eventually become a symbol of forgiveness. But it is certainly no longer just a sign; experience has transformed it into a most powerful symbol.

A symbol may also, through time, lose its meaning and become merely a sign once again. At one time "Watergate" referred only to a prestigious building complex in Washington, D.C. However, the 1972 break-in of the Democratic Headquarters located in this building began a scandalous period in our country's history. For those of us who remember that period, the word *Watergate* is an emotional trigger. But with time, it will eventually become devoid of emotion and join the list of terms that students of United States history will be required to memorize.

Symbols are based on human experience and are integral to our various traditions. We have national traditions, school and professional traditions, ethnic and family traditions. And we have religious traditions such as liturgy, where we come together to praise God as a community; in spite of the diversity among us, we are united in symbol. Symbols can unite people—even when everyone does not interpret them the same way.

Symbols occur in all areas of our existence, distinguishing humanity as an intelligent and communal species. Most organizations use symbols: special handshakes or salutes, sayings or mottoes, flags, ceremonies and rituals, uniforms, hats, personal gear. Some are signs of membership in the group; others are distinctly symbolic.

An example of a national symbol is the United States flag. As a piece of material it has little intrinsic value; yet if someone throws it to the ground and walks on it, that action will evoke a strong emotional response in many people. Why? Certainly not because something of great monetary value has been ruined. Rather, the emotional response occurs because the flag symbolizes our country.

The sports world overflows with traditions and rituals that can be symbols for us, such as the Olympic Parade of Athletes, a homecoming parade and game, the Special Olympics oath, tennis players shaking hands after a match, runners doing a victory lap, a celebrity throwing out the first ball at the game.

Even spectators have rituals and traditions, such as standing and singing the National Anthem; participating in the traditional reactions when "our team" takes to the playing field or enters the arena, scores, receives an unfavorable call, makes an impressive play; participating in a "wave"; taking a seventh-inning stretch; wearing the colors of the team.

Our holiday celebrations also include rituals that may be symbolic: making New Year's resolutions; sending Valentine cards; attending a sunrise Easter service; putting flowers and flags on graves for Memorial Day; watching a Fourth of July parade and fireworks display; giving treats to Halloween-costumed visitors; eating Thanksgiving Day dinner with family and friends; giving Christmas gifts; attending a New Year's Eve party.

Each of us could name traditions we could abandon with little regret; for others these same traditions could not be discontinued without the event being celebrated losing some of its integrity. Symbols, rituals and traditions help form us and define who we are. To the extent that we depend on these symbols for our ongoing identity we will remain attached to them.

One of the biggest adjustments in marriage is the intermingling of symbols and traditions from two different families. How many times the new bride or groom says, "In my family we always...." These are not merely occasions for humor; these are examples of the importance of symbols and traditions in defining and describing who we are.

Personal symbols can differ from one person to another. Something deeply symbolic to one person may be quite meaningless to another. Each individual's list of symbols is unique, for the basis of symbol is personal experience. Through our experience we make a personal identification with a symbol. The symbol becomes part of us, part of our history, and helps form our identity. Through the symbol a continuity is established with the past that continues on through the present and projects into the future. In this way the symbol becomes sacred to us.

Whenever a symbol is chosen by the community, it has intense power. Then the symbol represents not only our own experience but the communal experience of those with whom we are in union.

In Scripture water is a symbol of life, death, victory, defeat and much more. "In the beginning" we have the waters of chaos, then Noah and the flood, Moses and the parting of the Red Sea, the baptism of Jesus, the water turned into wine and so on. Water, whether pictured, described or used in a ritual, can convey directly opposing realities or truths, completely frustrating any attempt to "define" what it symbolizes for everyone.

Because a symbol is based on experience, it may acquire a multiplicity of meanings. For example, all of us encounter water in our life, yet what a variety of messages it carries.

Water is a symbol of:	*Through our experience of:*
life	growing plants and flowers
destruction	surviving a flood
refreshment	drinking when thirsty
work	doing tasks that need water
new life	giving birth
relaxation	vacationing at the shore
death	losing a friend through drowning
serenity	watching a sunset over a calm lake
turbulence	seeing a rushing stream or cascading waterfall
cleansing	washing with water
play	cavorting in a lake, stream, ocean
pain	being scalded
hunger	assuaging hunger pangs with water
force	canoeing both upstream and downstream
pleasure	taking an invigorating shower or relaxing bath
energy	observing a power-generating dam
food	eating fish or seafood
abundance	flooding that nourishes fields
beauty	observing a seascape
disappointment	having an outdoor event spoiled by rain
majesty	viewing waterfalls or oceans

Similar lists of varied and even contradictory meanings could be constructed for other things often used as symbols, such as bread, oil, light, banquet, mountain, family, sun, gold, song, sowing, birth, breath and so on. For each of these we could construct a list of possible meanings. But what is real to us is our own experience, along with our reactions to those experiences.

That's what makes symbols so powerful. Symbols have the potential to encourage or discourage, renew or devastate, awaken or numb, stimulate or dishearten. Symbols can make memories come alive; symbols can transform us.

▶ *"Approaching the church for a friend's funeral I saw that the entire complex was surrounded by a ten-foot high wrought-iron fence set in concrete, with just one small open gate. During the service the presider never acknowledged the presence of visitors. Many older people, fearing the difficulty of walking in the cemetery, left immediately after the funeral. Only after the committal did the presider acknowledge the presence of anyone—that's when those of us who had endured were invited for refreshments. That fence was a powerful symbol of the inhospitality of the faith community."*

▶ *"The response of some Catholics to the change of the Friday abstinence regulation was amazing—and dismaying. It became apparent that not eating meat on Friday was at the very core of their faith! That was how they defined being Catholic!"*

Using Symbols

The importance of symbols in our worship testifies to our belief that public worship is not just an intellectual experience. Symbols are integral to worship since it is only through symbols that we can speak the unspeakable, transcend physical reality to a deeper reality, unite contradictory realities, express our deepest longings, give meaning to life beyond what is seen, express love or universal truths, attempt to describe God.

Symbols can be so powerful that people have willingly gone to their death rather than perform a symbolic ritual such as bowing before a person or thing or eating forbidden food. And a clash of symbols produces the most emotional battles, as evidenced in religious wars. For centuries peoples have waged bitter, cruel wars over the area called the Holy Land—land sacred to several religious groups. People identify with that land as a symbol of their religious beliefs: "If my group does not possess what I consider sacred, then somehow both my faith and I are lessened."

Symbols focus our attention not on the symbols themselves, but on all they represent; they speak eloquently to our feelings, senses, memories and desires. Presiders at symbolic rituals need to be theologians not only of the head but also of the heart.

Once we, as presiders, develop a feel for symbols, we can use them effectively in our liturgies. As we choose objects and rituals we ask: Does it have historic or scriptural meaning or meanings? If it does, what are they? Is it a symbol today—or merely a sign? What are possible

CONSIDER

Have you ever observed the misuse of symbols? When? What was your response?

How important is it for you to know the "correct" meaning of a symbol? Why?

What are some ways that a presider can effectively use symbols? How comfortable are you in doing these things?

What are the main symbols in the rites at which you will be presiding? What do they symbolize to you? How do you plan to use them?

PRAYER
p**R**EPARATION
pr**A**CTICE
pra**Y**er

Every word, gesture, movement, object, appointment must be real in the sense that it is our own. It must come from the deepest understanding of ourselves (not careless, phony, counterfeit, pretentious, exaggerated, etc.).... Renewal requires the opening up of our symbols, especially the fundamental ones of bread and wine, water, oil, the laying on of hands, until we can experience all of them as authentic and appreciate their symbolic value. (Environment and Art in Catholic Worship, #14, 15)

meanings of the symbol today?

It has been said that the devil teaches us to trivialize our own experiences. Using symbols and allowing them to speak affirms everyone's ability to name and claim his or her own experience.

Some common errors in using symbols are:

- assuming that everyone is touched by the same symbols;
- attempting to control symbols;
- not empowering others to believe in their own experience;
- over-explaining symbols;
- failing to explain on those rare occasions when a symbol requires explanation.

When we explain a symbol we immediately limit its meaning. The effective use of symbols is an implicit act of faith in the Holy Spirit. Symbols need not be interpreted the same way by everyone. A transparent presider lets symbols and rituals speak for themselves.

A short list of possible symbols would include the following: light, meal, oil, food, banquet, water, sun, moon, candles, children, parents, birth, death, milk, breast, dying, song, giving birth, barrenness, singing, breath, wind, stone, silence, language, speech, words, growth, plants, animals, flowers, feminine attributes of God, masculine attributes of God, cross, crucifix, rising sun, wealth, gold, sowing, harvest, growing fields, touch, hill, valley, mountaintop, desert, religious habits, vestments, the sign of the cross, the lighting of candles, the extinguishing of candles....

▶ *"I belong to an ecumenical women's group. We rotate hosting the meetings, and the host plans the opening prayer or ritual. We had been meeting for over a year when someone observed that the Protestants always opened the meeting with a Scripture reading while the Catholics, who may or may not include Scripture in the opening, always included a ritual. We Catholics are ritual people!"*

▶ *"Working in a large company means I don't know all the other employees. But what a powerful experience it is on Ash Wednesday to see all the darkened foreheads among my coworkers! So many people claiming their Catholic identity—it's inspiring!"*

▶ *"John was a well-liked cantor and choir member for many years and the shocking news of his sudden death spread rapidly through our faith community. Every choir member came to sing for his funeral. When people entered the worship space they responded with a gasp at the sight before them: the full robed choir standing in their places while in front of them was an empty chair—with John's choir robe draped over it."*

▶ *"Since I travel in my work, I attend liturgies in many places. When our family moved to a new city, we looked around before joining a parish. You know what convinced me that we had found the right one? The eucharistic ministers and the priest serve the community first before they receive communion. That spoke to me of the spirit of service in the community—and that's where we joined!"*

▶ *"I am always deeply touched by the veneration of the cross on Good Friday. The diverse ways people use in reverencing the cross represent such different emotions: gratitude, love, respect, sorrow, guilt, awe. Some kiss the feet of the corpus, some touch the wood with their fingertips, some stand nearby and make the sign of the cross on themselves, some approach from a distance on their knees, some bow deeply, some embrace the cross. And I? I am most affected by the diversity of the responses."*

▶ *"The Easter Vigil began outside. We gathered around the huge 'new fire' as our ancestors must have gathered around the campfire. The lector stepped forward and told the creation story from memory. How many times I have heard those words—'In the beginning...'—yet listening to the storyteller, it was as if I were hearing them for the first time!"*

Sacraments and Sacramental Actions

The Church has been inspired to recognize and formalize, over a long period of time, seven sacraments. These sacraments make tangible in the world the presence of God's grace, and we who have been baptized are representatives of that grace.

There have been occasions in our history when these sacraments were regarded in a manner bordering on the superstitious; there have been times when people have focused on the magic of priestly hands while dismissing the action of the community, the disposition of the individuals involved, or even God's mercy and love.

We have come to realize that often a sacrament is a ritual action recognizing what already exists. This does not lessen the sacramental action or minimize our need for that ritual, for we still need it to affirm what is, so that the reality may become ever more real.

For example, we who are baptized have been initiated into the Body of Christ. Each time we participate in the eucharistic liturgy and receive communion we receive the transforming Body of Christ. We, who are the Body of Christ, receive the body and blood of Christ, each time affirming: We are the Body of Christ!

If we really believe that we are the Body of Christ, then many of our daily actions are outward expressions of God's love. Much of our life consists of possible sacramental rituals. We constantly have opportunities to express love, to be life-giving and life-sustaining, to bring God's grace to others. Consider how these actions might be sacramental:

- preparing and serving a meal;
- caring for a sick child or friend;
- bringing beauty and music and dance to the world;
- teaching;
- giving birth;
- bringing the gospel message to the world;
- earning money to provide for ourself and others;
- expressing love through sex;
- being friendly and gracious and kind;
- learning about this vast universe that God created;
- praying for others;
- feeding an infant;
- entering into the silence that is God;

CONSIDER

What is your definition of sacrament or sacramental?

How do you feel about being described as a member of "a chosen race, a royal priesthood, a holy nation" (1 Peter 2:9)?

What do you do in your daily life that reflects God's goodness, mercy, care or love?

How do you regard presiding?

Thus, for well-disposed members of the faithful, the effect of the liturgy of the sacraments and sacramentals is that almost every event in their lives is made holy by divine grace that flows from the paschal mystery of Christ's passion, death, and resurrection, the fount from which all sacraments and sacramentals draw their power.... there is hardly any proper use of material things that cannot thus be directed toward human sanctification and the praise of God. (Constitution on the Sacred Liturgy, #61)

- being creative;
- encouraging and nurturing others;
- bringing laughter to others;
- celebrating the sacred in our lives;
- working in the healing arts;
- being joyous;
- expressing reverence for nature and the gifts of creation;
- consoling those who mourn;
- caring for children, for the elderly;
- bringing God to others;
- building community;
- finding God's presence all around us;
- helping others;
- showing respect for all living beings;
- listening;
- being Christ to the world.

These actions, integral elements of our daily life, carry the possibility of being sacramental.

▶ *"The neighboring Baptist minister called me recently, having heard good things about our foot-washing ritual on Holy Thursday. He wanted to know how to do it—and I didn't know where to start! Our faith community began to set the stage on Ash Wednesday and continued our preparation throughout Lent. The foot-washing is part of the three-day celebration of Triduum; it is surrounded by music and drama and dance and Scripture and other rituals; it touches us because of what we know we will celebrate the next day, Good Friday; its powerful symbolism is connected with its place in the Paschal Mystery. How can all that be conveyed in the description of a ritual?"*

Our Need for Ritual and Symbol

We need ritual! We need familiar, common ground upon which to meet our neighbors and build community. "Hello. How are you?" "Fine! And how are you?"

We need the familiar, the routine, to recognize the passage of time, the milestones we pass on the continuing spiral of life. "Happy birthday to you, happy birthday to you...."

We need the familiar, the routine, the common ground to recognize our past—as individuals, as family, as a faith community, as a nation, as a global village. "Whenever the family gathers, Grandpa tells those too-familiar stories, Auntie has her invariable treasury of jokes, the kids have their same questions."

We need the routine, the never-changing, to give us the confidence to encounter the new, the ever-changing. "I have my morning routine: getting up, dressing, eating, driving to work—all automatic. I don't begin thinking until I get to my desk."

We need the familiar, the routine, to give us the strength and courage to deal with the unfamiliar and changing aspects of life. "We're all gathering at Mom's for Thanksgiving. It will be the usual: the Thanksgiving Day parade, dinner, TV football—and my pumpkin pies!"

We need the familiar, the routine, the solid ground from which to be launched into the future—the future of this day, the future of this life, the future of this faith community, the future of this world. "The politicking and campaigning, the voting, the swearing in and inauguration, all part of the ongoing history of this country. No sooner does one cycle end than another begins."

We need the familiar, the routine, to prepare us to encounter our God. "The Lord be with you." "And also with you."

We need the familiar rituals to unite us, through liturgy that overflows with spiritual meaning, into a caring community. "Birth and baptism, the sacramental and communal life, the dying and burial—all ritualized into the Paschal Mystery."

We need the familiar rituals to put us, the assembly, at ease so that we may listen each other into prayer and worship. "The liturgical year—the seasons and feasts and readings come and go and return again. But I change with time, and so all are ever new."

We need the familiar rituals so that, even if we do not all interpret them the same way, we are united into community.

▶ *"In my years of being on our parish's RCIA team, I've heard many stories about why people want to join the Catholic Church. But the reason that comes up most often? It's because of our liturgies and sacramental system!"*

CHAPTER 5

The World of Liturgy

The main focus of the liturgical renewal is not revised rites but change in people's hearts. Presiders need to be theologians not only of the head but also of the heart. The music, poetry, art and dance of liturgy comprise the heart language; through culturally influenced symbol and ritual we declare our faith and unite our community with the larger Church; through the symbols and rituals of liturgy hearts are changed. Everything in the world affects liturgy. And everything in liturgy makes a statement about our faith. In liturgy, everything speaks!

O Most Bounteous God!
You have sanctified our world with beauty.
Our universe dances,
makes music,
stirs us to tears with its splendor!
Inspire us in our worship of you!
Direct us in what we do—
that the sound and sight
and movement and touch of our liturgies
may be pleasing to you
and reveal yet more of you to us.
We ask this in the name of Jesus the Christ,
who sang and danced and prayed among us,
and who is Lord for ever and ever. Amen.

The Liturgical Year

An integral part of the Catholic Church's ritual observance is the liturgical year. This celebration of seasons and feasts dramatically presents our history and theology, our faith in one another and in God, our hope in one another and in God, our love for one another and for God.

The liturgical year celebrates the events of Christ's birth and ministry, death and resurrection; our historical roots as described in the Hebrew Scriptures; events in the early Church; God's goodness and presence in the cycles of time, through the days and the seasons; God's presence in the today and now of salvation history.

In the liturgical cycle the Church not only tells the stories of our past but makes these events present for us today. This cycle of seasons has an intentional repetition of stories, music and rituals; through this repetition we anticipate them, celebrate them and then remember them, knowing they will return yet again.

Through the repetition, the familiarity, the perennial tensions, each season moves into us and we become one with that season. The liturgical year provides us with communal experiences, helps us think and feel as a community. These yearly rituals affirm who we are as they intersect the rhythms of our lives.

CONSIDER

How do you mark the passage of time?

What are some of the significant before-and-after events in your life that help you remember when things occurred?

What are some of the significant before-and-after events in Scripture?

When are you most aware of the liturgical year? How? Why?

Are there any feasts that are especially important in your faith community? What are they? Why and how are they celebrated?

Are there any feasts that are especially important to you or your family? What

PRAYER
PR**E**PARATION
PR**A**CTICE
PRA**Y**ER

are they? Why and how do you celebrate them?

How would you find the assigned readings for a particular Sunday of the year? For a particular feast day?

Within the cycle of a year, moreover, the Church unfolds the whole mystery of Christ, from his incarnation and birth until his ascension, the day of Pentecost, and the expectation of blessed hope and of the Lord's return. Recalling thus the mysteries of redemption, the Church opens to the faithful the riches of the Lord's powers and merits, so that these are in some way made present in every age, in order that the faithful may lay hold on them and be filled with saving grace. (Constitution on the Sacred Liturgy, #102)

Through the readings, prayers and rituals of the liturgical year we are affirmed as enfleshed, embodied spirits who rejoice, mourn, forgive and need forgiveness; through this liturgical repetition we are reminded that we are creatures of a loving Creator; we are the Body of Christ, yet ever in need of conversion. Through the liturgical year we are reminded of the mysteries of death-and-resurrection in our lives. We are reminded that we are earthly inhabitants of a vast universe, yet still members of the one family of God.

The liturgical seasons are related both to what has occurred in the past and to what is to come. Through the cycle of seasons and feasts we received our faith; through the cycle of seasons we hand on our faith. The seasons connect us with the greater Church.

As the liturgical year passes we see that each season or feast has its own focus, mood, themes, colors, music, spirit. A season or feast does not have a theme thrust upon it that is to be carried out in the environment or music or preaching. Instead, through study of the Scriptures and rituals and traditions, the student of liturgy discovers within that season or feast a spirit, or perhaps the Spirit, speaking to us now. We do not impose a theme or a mood; rather we seek God's presence within the season and within the liturgy. We look for the Advent within us, the Resurrection within us, the between-times within us; we look for the rhythm of the year.

All our liturgies, whether the faith community's Sunday eucharistic celebration, or a small gathering for Evening Prayer, are celebrations of the greater Church—the People of God. The scriptural readings of the liturgical year unite us with the greater Church; our public worship, no matter how prestigious or seemingly insignificant, is a statement of our tradition and faith, affirming us as the Body of Christ.

In addition to the great seasons and feasts celebrated in the liturgical year we honor the saints, that "cloud of witnesses," who have gone before us and have passed on to us their faith. The liturgical year also celebrates devotional feasts such as those honoring a particular aspect of an event in salvation history or a specific title of God or Mary.

We also recognize national influences in our lives by celebrating national and regional occasions: Memorial Day, the Fourth of July, Thanksgiving Day, Martin Luther King Day and so on. We recognize the feasts celebrated and memorials commemorated by the other "Peoples of the Book"—the Jews and the Muslims—such as the Jewish High Holy Days, Hanukkah, the Holocaust Memorial Day and the observance of Ramadan.

Because of local custom, ethnic tradition, a patron saint of the parish or faith community, regional influence and other factors, every locality or community may have celebrations of special significance: a Hispanic community that celebrates the feast of Our Lady of Guadalupe—December 12th; an Irish community that celebrates Saint Patrick's Day—March 17th; a faith community served by a Franciscan order that honors Saint Francis on his feast day—October 4th; a community that gathers for worship at Annunciation Church will probably honor Mary on the feast of the Annunciation—March 25th.

The liturgical calendar is composed of events that have fixed dates, such as Christmas and the feast of Mary's Assumption on August 15th, as well as events that have variable dates, such as Easter and the First Sunday of Advent.

Lest the feasts of the saints take precedence over the feasts commemorating the very mysteries of salvation, many of them should be left to be celebrated by a particular Church or nation or religious family; only those should be extended to the universal Church that commemorate saints of truly universal significance. (Constitution on the Sacred Liturgy, #111)

Information concerning the specific celebration and Scripture readings for each day of the liturgical cycle is readily available in various sources: *The Ordo (or The Order of) Prayers in the Liturgy of the Hours and Celebration of the Eucharist (YEAR) for* (diocese); missalettes; liturgical calendars; numerous liturgy helps available through publishers, worship centers, liturgy offices and other sources.

These aids list the assigned Scripture readings in the lectionary for each day of the liturgical year. In addition to the readings for the liturgical year, time and tradition has established certain colors for the celebration of feasts and seasons. These colors are reflected in vestments and the worship environment. A lay presider does not use vesture color, but it is important to be aware of the significance of color in our liturgy and in our liturgical environment.

▶ *"Each year our parish provides us with a list of the Scripture readings for every day. Most days I read the assigned Scripture as part of my morning prayer. If I later hear those readings proclaimed at liturgy, I always seem to get more out of them. I also find I've become aware of how the cycles are arranged—like when we focus on the different Gospels."*

▶ *"I was never aware of the liturgical year until I joined our parish's liturgy board. Before that, I was only vaguely aware of the change of seasons—but I never 'felt' them. Now, as we routinely plan one or two seasons ahead, while evaluating our observances of the past season and celebrating the present one, I see the overall flow of time and seasons. It gives me a sense of place within time and I now experience each season more deeply."*

The Liturgical Seasons

Advent. The liturgical year begins with Advent, approximately four weeks before Christmas. Advent always has four Sundays and between three and four weeks. Advent does not initiate the celebration of Christmas, but focuses attention on the preparation for Christmas.

Advent is a time of waiting and yearning, of joyful anticipation, of silence and emptiness, of looking within, of preparing for the coming of the Cosmic Christ. The music of Advent reflects the mood of Advent; the music of Advent is not Christmas carols!

The liturgical color of Advent is indigo or violet, the color of the predawn darkness; it is Mary's color as she is clothed with the night and adorned with stars.

Christmas Season. The celebration of the feast of the Incarnation begins with the vigil liturgy of Christmas and extends through Epiphany to the feast of the Baptism of Our Lord. We are celebrating not just the birth of the baby Jesus, but what the Incarnation means to humanity. We are celebrating the Christ present in us who are the Mystical Body!

Epiphany is the fullness of the Incarnation; it is the celebration of God-Made-Flesh; it is the manifestation of God to everyone; it is the proclamation of the gospel message of justice and love to all. We celebrate Emmanuel—God with us! The liturgical color of the Christmas

CONSIDER

What do you regard as the advantages of observing the liturgical year? The disadvantages?

What are your favorite liturgical feasts? Why? What is your favorite season? Why?

How does the liturgical year affirm the human experience?

What is your experience of Triduum? Why is Triduum considered a single feast? Why is it considered the high point of the liturgical year?

What is your experience of the Paschal Mystery?

During the course of the year the different mysteries of redemption are celebrated at Mass so that in some way they are made present. Each feast and season has its own spirit and its own music. (Music in Catholic Worship, #19)

season is either white or gold.

Ordinary Time. The name "Ordinary Time" can be misleading. It is not ordinary in the sense of routine and boring, for no season filled with the tales of Christ's miracles and endlessly intriguing parables could ever be described as routine! It is not empty time; rather it is time of proclaiming, through word and deed, what we celebrate. Ordinary Time reminds us of the sacramentality of everyday life. As we hear the story of salvation history proclaimed we realize that "now" is a most extraordinary time!

The number of weeks of the after-Christmas Ordinary Time varies each year. Ordinary Time continues until the beginning of Lent on Ash Wednesday.

The music and symbols of Ordinary Time reflect the Scripture readings, the gospel challenge, the Christian life. The liturgical color for Ordinary Time is green, the color of hope, of life, of nature's awakening and rebirth, of growth.

Lent. Lent, which begins on Ash Wednesday, originally was set aside to prepare new members to join the Christian community; gradually it became a time of penance, almsgiving and prayer.

Today we recognize the importance of Lent both in preparing incoming members of the faith community and in revitalizing the present community. As the community prepares for the baptism of its newest members, we renew our own baptismal commitments.

Lent continues for six full weeks and concludes at sundown on Holy Thursday. The color of Lent is purple and the symbols suggest conversion, baptism preparation, sin and forgiveness, faith and commitment, new beginnings.

Triduum. Triduum means three days. Using the Jewish custom of beginning the day at sundown, the three days begin on Holy Thursday evening and continue to Evening Prayer on Easter. These high holy days are celebrated with the services of Holy Thursday evening, Good Friday, the Vigil on Holy Saturday and Easter. Each day has its own story, mood and focus of celebration.

The Easter Vigil service on Saturday evening, the high point of the entire liturgical year, overflows with rituals. During this liturgy the paschal candle that will be used throughout the coming year is both blessed and lighted. We celebrate this liturgy of the resurrection by receiving new members into our community, thereby renewing us as community and committing ourselves to be accountable to these who are young in the faith.

The significance of the one feast of Triduum, which we need three days to celebrate, cannot be overemphasized. We do not relive the passion, death and resurrection of Christ, but rather enter into the Paschal Mystery, the core of our belief as Christians. It is difficult to understand or appreciate the remainder of the liturgical year if we do not fully celebrate Triduum.

Easter Season. The Easter season begins on Easter Sunday evening and continues through Pentecost. Forty days were spent preparing for Triduum and now fifty days are needed to celebrate the event!

Many of the symbols of Easter emphasize new life (the newly

baptized, the empty tomb) as well as Christ as the light of the world and the cross now glorified. The Church commemorates the Easter victory with the color white.

The liturgical color of Pentecost, which ends our season of Easter, is vibrant red—the color of the flames of the Holy Spirit on that first transforming Pentecost.

Ordinary Time. Ordinary Time now resumes and the counting of the Sundays in Ordinary Time continues from the Ordinary Time that preceded Lent. As before, the color of this season is green and the symbols are taken from the Scripture readings, the sacramentality of the Christian life, the gospel challenge.

Ordinary Time continues through the feast of Christ the King on the last Sunday before Advent.

And then, it all begins again.

▶ *"When I lector I like to think about all the places in the world where those same Scriptures are being read that very day! In my parish community we are listening to these readings in common with Catholics and Episcopalians and Lutherans around the world. In churches and chapels and cathedrals, huts and homes, and in the open air, lectors and presiders are reading these Scriptures in languages and dialects that I couldn't even identify! Yet it is a bond uniting us—and a reminder that we are all one people."*

▶ *"I am an Ordinary Time Christian. My life—and my faith—are not composed of momentous events or extremes of emotion or noteworthy spiritual experiences. This is fine, for I find in Ordinary Time a quiet simplicity, a joyful and sustaining faith, and a deep, deep love that assures me of God's constant presence."*

Sacred Space

CONSIDER

In what way is all space sacred?

When have you entered a space—and known immediately that it was sacred? What made it sacred?

Is there a space—not generally considered sacred—that is sacred to you? Where? Why do you consider it sacred?

What is your answer to the person who says that nature is a better place for praying than a church?

What part does assembly or community have in making a space sacred for you?

At times we enter a space and immediately gasp for breath; we know this is sacred space. In this space we feel God's presence, we hear the echoes of all the prayers prayed there, we are touched by the creativity of those who have enhanced this space with their artistic endeavors, we hear the continuing reverberations of the hymns sung there; in this space we are surrounded by a "cloud of witnesses," part of the community of believers.

This is indeed sacred space, made so by love and by lovers, by faith and by believers—and we are awed and humbled. In such a space we do not have to be reminded to move reverently; in such an environment prayer comes easier and ritual seems natural.

Space becomes sacred through the action of God—either in the past or in the present, or through the faith of those who have gathered there in the past; space can also become sacred through our faith and our actions in preparation and in gathering there now.

This is the ideal, where we come to encounter the sacred; this is where we celebrate community. In this ideal space, the environment professes our theology and assists us in our worship.

All prayer, including public prayer, is affected by the environment.

The worship service held in a magnificent cathedral takes on a different character than the same service held in a simple white clapboard chapel; music befitting a campfire service seems inappropriate at morning prayer in a retreat house; the words spoken in a school gymnasium seem to lack authenticity when repeated in a hospice setting.

The environment includes many elements. The space in which we pray and the seating arrangement in that space influence the worship; the artistic enhancement and lighting of that space affect prayer; everything used in the ritual and everything seen, felt, tasted, heard, touched, smelled influence that worship.

Often the lay presider has little input as to either the place of worship or the liturgical environment. A community makes use of the worship space it has, rejoicing in its strengths, tolerating its weaknesses. In other instances the presider may have total responsibility for the environment.

Since environment is such a powerful influence, it needs to be considered when planning a liturgy. Some spaces are not conducive to public worship; when facing such a challenge, a presider needs to understand how to help create an environment suitable for prayer.

► *"I define sacred space as that which gives both me and the assembly a jump-start on prayer."*

► *"I always feel much closer to God in a woods or by a lake or at the seacoast than I do in most churches. All those statues and pictures seem so dead! To me they are cold and lifeless. But nature is alive! Nature surrounds me, speaks to me, touches me, interacts with me—and that's much more like God!"*

► *"When I was in Israel I visited the Church of the Annunciation, built over the location where the Annunciation supposedly occurred. Whether that is true was irrelevant for me. When I entered I was engulfed with the feeling of faith that persisted there, the abiding and overwhelming faith of all the believers who had been there before me."*

Architecture for Worship

The Second Vatican Council resulted in great transition within the Church. Changes had been initiated in both theology and practice, and implementing those changes brought about much upheaval. New rituals and prayer models were tried; many were discarded while others survived with significant revision. New hymns and types of singing and instrumentation were tried; in time, many were judged of little value, while others were refined. New approaches in religious education were tried; most were much revised. Gradually, through trial and error, through revision and refinement, the better and more effective hymns and rituals and religious education programs surfaced.

The same process must be endured when it comes to the art and architecture of worship spaces—but with added complications. Though a faith community may discard a parish hymnal because its music no longer serves the community, discarding an entire building is not so easily accomplished! Thus, what was achieved musically and ritually in ten or twenty years may take many decades in worship space design.

Because the assembly gathers in the presence of God to celebrate his saving deeds, liturgy's climate is one of awe, mystery, wonder, reverence, thanksgiving and praise. So it cannot be satisfied with anything less than the beautiful in its environment and in all its artifacts, movements, and appeals to the senses. Admittedly difficult to define, the beautiful is related to the sense of the numinous, the holy. Where there is evidently no care for this, there is an environment basically unfriendly to mystery and awe, an environment too casual, if not careless, for the liturgical action. In a world dominated by science and technology, liturgy's quest for the beautiful is a particularly necessary contribution to full and balanced human life. (Environment and Art in Catholic Worship, #34)

When churches are to be built, let great care be taken that they are well suited to celebrating liturgical services and to bringing about the active participation of the faithful. (Constitution on the Sacred Liturgy, #124)

CONSIDER

What were some short-lived fads that followed the Second Vatican Council? Why did they not survive?

What were some new hymns that were popular following the Council that are no longer used? Why did they not survive?

What do you like best about the traditional-style church? What do you dislike?

What emotions do you experience in a traditional-style church?

What do you like best about modern-style churches? What do you dislike?

What emotions do you experience in a modern-style church?

In architecture there is much truth in the saying that form follows function. The design of a worship space depends upon what is to be done there and what theological statements it is to make. Traditional church architecture was developed within the theology of the time and was influenced by the function worship had within that theology.

Much of the theology stated in traditional worship spaces still holds: awe before the majesty of God, reverence for holy actions and holy objects, the recognition of humanity's brokenness and limitations before the unlimited and holy Divinity, wonder at the ever-expanding history of God's involvement with humanity, fascination with the stories of the saints who have gone before us.

Other aspects of traditional worship spaces needed to be changed, however. We no longer have a sharp distinction between the sanctuary and the congregation. No longer is the world divided into sacred and secular realities. The priest is no longer the main focus; we recognize that the assembly is now the main minister of liturgy and of music. God is present not only in the communion elements, but also in the ministers, in the Scriptures, and in each person; thus we no longer center on the tabernacle as the sign of Christ present. Because Scripture is more prominent in the revised rites, the ambo and the altar balance one another in the sanctuary area.

The beauty of the traditional church building—the arches and spires that reach toward heaven, the stained glass and statues and artwork, are moving reminders of our rich past, of the talents, gifts and sacrifices of so many people, of our God of beauty. But in recognition of how much worshipers are influenced by the environment, Vatican II has challenged the faithful to seek and appreciate different types of beauty as well, worship spaces that give voice to a new theology. As to exactly what that space looks like, feels like—the answer is that it is still transition time.

▶ *"When we remodeled our church we added a gathering space. It's a wonderful addition, for it conveys hospitality as soon as you enter the building. We have coffee there after liturgy while we visit with friends, meet new people, build community. It's amazing how that space has affected our parish!"*

▶ *"I love to meditate in a traditional church. The statues and stained glass all inspire me. However, I prefer to worship in a newer building where I can focus on the liturgy and on the living saints around me."*

▶ *"I don't like statues in church. They distract me from recognizing the Christ of today. I need to see the saints in the pew with me and those across the aisle and that entire saintly choir!"*

▶ *"I still prefer the traditional churches. I understand that we are all made in the image of God and I work hard trying to see Christ in everyone. But when I go to church I want to see statues of the saints and stained glass scenes and gold and silver chalices; I want to be reminded of the mystery and majesty of the Divine Holy One!"*

▶ *"I've always been fascinated by places like Stonehenge and Easter Island and what they tell us about the religious practices of people long ago. As our Catholic theology continues to develop our worship spaces will change too. Will there come a time when people will visit ancient Gothic-style churches and wonder about the theology of the people who worshiped there? What sacred places of today will become the Stonehenges of the future?"*

Environment and Theology

Environment, like everything else involved in worship, effectively teaches and ratifies theology. For example, note which areas of the worship space we enhance. In the past, most of the artistic enhancement was done in the sanctuary—a space physically separated from the body of the church by steps and a communion rail. While it gave honor to the presence of Christ in the tabernacle, it ignored the presence of Christ in the assembly—the Body of Christ! It recognized the ministry of the presider but dismissed the ministry of the assembly.

The variety of architecture that has emerged following the Council testifies to the crucial interaction of form, function and theology. The enhancement of the environment, too, needs to state that the believing assembly is worth honoring. In many worship spaces today the entire area is considered by the environmental artist. Thus banners, flowers and streamers may be used throughout the worship space to recognize the assembly as the People of God and the primary minister of the liturgy.

This attention to the worship space not only answers the needs of function, not only adds beauty, but expresses theology through the arrangement of the space, placement of furniture, lighting, seating arrangement and other details.

When we gather for liturgy in settings other than the parish worship space, these elements are also important. As an example, some worship spaces allow for groups to be seated in a circle. This arrangement recognizes that the liturgy is the work of the people, emphasizes the importance of the ministry of the assembly, minimizes the exclusive focus upon an altar area or presider, acknowledges equality yet diversity of ministry, makes shared collaborative leadership easier and honors God's presence in each of us. All this can be conveyed through the seating arrangement.

▶ *"Whenever I preside for a children's service or one at the nursing home, I try to have people gather around me in a circle. That arrangement connects me not only to those gathered there, but also to the ancient Hebrews sitting around the evening campfire telling stories. They told and remembered those stories so well that the tales were handed down for generations."*

Furniture

The Table of the Lord. The altar table represents Christ. We gather around this table and we come to this table to be fed. We do not ordinarily place things on the table, except for what is actually being used during the eucharistic liturgy. The altar is not to be regarded as a convenient place for either storage or decoration. This is why floor candle holders are usually used in a permanent worship space.

CONSIDER

How would you describe the difference in design of pre-Vatican II churches and those designed after the Council?

What theology is taught by the way your parish worship space is arranged? By the way it is decorated or enhanced?

How do you feel as a member of the assembly when seated in a circle for worship? In the more traditional seating?

How do you feel as a presider when seated in a circle? In the more traditional seating?

How do you feel about services in a funeral home? A meeting room at the parish administration center? A nursing home? An outdoor setting?

CONSIDER

When you enter your faith community's worship space, what symbolizes Christ to you? Why? How does the altar table symbolize Christ?

The altar, the holy table, should be the most noble, the most beautifully designed and constructed table the community can provide (General Instruction, #259-270; Appendix to General Instruction, #263). It is the common table of the assembly, a symbol of the Lord, at which the presiding minister stands and upon which are placed the bread and wine and their vessels and the book. (Environment and Art in Catholic Worship, #71)

CONSIDER

What theologies are "taught" by how your assembly space is constructed? By its liturgical art? Is this what you want? If not, what can be done?

What theologies are "taught" by other spaces used for services? By their liturgical art? Is this what you want? If not, what can be done?

What theologies are "taught" by placement of flowers, candles, banners and other objects within these spaces?

Flowers, plants and trees—genuine, of course—are particularly apt for the decoration of liturgical space, since they are of nature, always discreet in their message, never cheap or tawdry or ill-made. Decoration should never im-

At a liturgy held in another location, we may have to adapt these principles somewhat, while still retaining as much reverence as possible for the altar table.

At the beginning and end of a liturgy the presider and other ministers reverence the altar, usually with a profound bow. Before, during and following the liturgy, the ministers reverence the altar whenever passing before it.

The Ambo. The ambo or lectern is the place of proclamation. It is worthy of honor and distinction because the word of God is proclaimed here.

Presider's Chair. A clarification must be made between *the* presider's chair and *a* presider's chair. In a temporary worship space, such as a funeral home or a classroom setting, a chair is usually available for use by the presider, ordained or lay. In such a situation, no restrictions would be placed upon the use of that presider's chair.

In a permanent worship space, such as a church, a special location is usually designated for the presider's chair. This is the place, during a eucharistic liturgy, where the priest presider sits during the Liturgy of the Word.

When a lay presider celebrates a Sunday Celebration in the Absence of a Priest, the rubrics specify that the lay presider does not use the presider's chair (see *Sunday Celebrations in the Absence of a Priest*, #24). Instead, another chair is placed nearby. This is a visual reminder to all that the assembly is not celebrating the complete eucharistic liturgy.

Enhancement

Another way of creating sacred space is by well-chosen and liturgically correct enhancement of the worship space. Colored cloths, draperies and banners are often used. These can be laid over furniture, hung at windows or along the walls, draped above the worship space. We let the colors themselves speak—no need for words or sayings; we creatively use color and movement, shape and line, aiming for simplicity. Even if we are not great artists, we do have to be sensitive to the power of environment as an influence on a worshiping community.

Candles have long held a special place in both liturgy and private devotions. Originally candles were used to provide light; they are now used for their aesthetic qualities. For example, we use candles around the altar and the ambo to mark them as especially significant and sacred. Other special candles include the paschal candle (lit at the Easter Vigil service and used throughout the year for funerals and other special occasions), baptismal candles, the sanctuary lamp indicating the divine sacramental presence in the tabernacle and vigil lights.

Other objects may also be used to enhance the worship space: fresh flowers, dried leaves or branches, greenery, cacti, rocks, sand, materials of various textures, weavings, bread, wine, water, oil, incense, candles, pottery, baskets, feathers, seashells, pine cones, ribbons, driftwood, bricks and so on.

We use natural materials whenever possible, avoiding artificial flowers, greenery and other objects unless practical considerations demand the use of some artificial items. Whatever is used, natural or

pede the approach to or the encircling of the altar or any of the ritual movement and action, but there are places in most liturgical spaces where it is appropriate and where it can be enhancing. The whole space is to be considered the arena of decoration, not merely the sanctuary. (Environment and Art in Catholic Worship, #102)

CONSIDER

What is the tradition in your parish concerning the handling of the articles used in ritual? What is especially revered?

What are some of the problems involved in presiding in a temporary worship space? How can you handle these challenges so as to assist the assembly in prayer?

artificial, needs to be of good quality.

We respond to particular situations and the opportunities they present. For example, at a nursing home liturgy we might use items belonging to residents—a crocheted scarf, embroidered cloth or knitted afghan—for the altar or ambo. We might invite residents to bring flowers from their rooms to decorate the sacred space during the liturgy. In a school setting we might incorporate pictures or other artwork done by the students. In a sickroom we might use favorite artwork of the patient or the family.

We are affected not only by the enhancement itself, but also by the creativity that goes into preparing the environment. The energy and creativity that exist there infuse energy back into the community. The symbols of our environment, if effectively used, engage our imagination and invite us to search inward and open ourselves to what happens in the worship space.

Ritual Objects

Also part of our environment are the various books and hymnals, worship aids, incense holders and other objects we use during the liturgy. All the articles used or viewed during liturgy communicate theology to us. The jeweled gold or silver chalices used during a eucharistic liturgy testify to our high regard for what is contained in those chalices. A pottery chalice reminds us that this is also a meal celebrated by ordinary Christians. A crystal chalice allows us to see what is contained in it, making visible what otherwise is hidden. Everything speaks!

When presiding, we regard all ritual objects with honor. While some of these objects may have been blessed, all of them become worthy of our respect because of their use in public prayer. Certainly we handle the lectionary carefully, because it contains the word of God. The worship aid, copied and assembled in the parish center for this liturgy only, is not sacred but its use during the liturgy demands that we not toss it around, fling it onto a chair, roll it into a cylinder or fidget with it during the readings. Such activity communicates disregard for an important item in the liturgy and suggests lack of respect for the liturgy itself.

▶ *"At our parish we recognize the blessedness of anointing. The sacred oils are carried reverently in procession on Holy Thursday and then, throughout the year—with the exception of Lent—they are displayed in the ambry, just inside the main doors of the worship space."*

▶ *"It happened at a ritual during a weekend retreat. We read the gospel story of the woman at the well, followed by a meditation on living water. In the midst of this solemn time, the presider passed around water for us to drink—in paper cups with choo-choo trains on them! Her rationale was that those were the cups on sale."*

Religious Art and Spiritual Art

As Christians we honor our heritage by telling our stories. But we also look with hope to the future, celebrating the reign of God still to come.

And we are deeply and lovingly committed to the reality, events and people of today.

We are the people of a God of beauty and mystery and unapproachable majesty, the God of the universe and of the Incarnation, a God who is always beyond our ability to describe or contain, yet a God who dwells within us. Somehow, our art is to convey all this.

In the consideration of environment and enhancement and creating sacred space, we need to make a distinction between religious art and spiritual or liturgical art.

Religious art portrays specific people or actions or events that are typically labeled religious. Religious art would include pictures or statues or representations of Christ, Mary or the saints, or events from Scripture or history. Speaking very generally, religious art is representational art, portraying a specific person or scene.

In contrast, spiritual art or liturgical art opens us up to mystery and encourages us to go inward to listen to the Spirit of God within us. It speaks to our imagination and creativity. It is not representational art, yet it speaks of truth beyond time or place or person.

Consider, for example, a candle set among stones and greenery with a backdrop in the colors of the season. While this is not religious art, it is spiritual art. It does not tell us what to think; it allows us to go inside ourselves and hear the voice of God within us. To use spiritual art is to rely upon the power of symbols, upon the ability of others to trust their own experience, and upon the activity of the Holy Spirit.

▶ *"'But what does it mean?' I am always amused—and a bit saddened—whenever I hear that question asked about our beautiful stained glass window, the work of a creative, gifted, liturgical artist. That window, which I believe was truly inspired, points to mystery-beyond-physical-representation. Every time I look at that design it says something different to me. That's why, when asked what it means, I answer with the question, 'What does it say to you today, here, now?'"*

Music in the Liturgy

The question is not, "Shall there be music?" but rather "Which music?" It is not, "Shall there be congregational singing?" but rather "What shall the congregation sing?" We do not have to explain why there is singing. Just as the assembly is the main minister of liturgy, so, too, the assembly is the primary minister of music. Singing in the liturgy is integral to the assembly's worship. The assembly bonds together in the act of making music.

Music helps to create an atmosphere; it speaks where and when words cannot and communicates our deepest feelings. Music is healing and unifying. It is the "memory keeper" of our tradition. It enhances the celebration and adds beauty to the liturgy. Music can go beyond culture, language, time and place. It is a universal language. It forms a bridge from the human to the divine. It has the power to stir memories and passionate emotions and allows us to praise God in ways that go beyond mere words.

Singing is a liturgical act; it is a communal response to God. Because we sing as members of the Body of Christ, liturgical music must be good,

CONSIDER

What kind of representational or religious art do you prefer? Is there a special time or situation when it seems most appropriate? Why?

What kind of liturgical or spiritual art do you prefer? Is there a special time or situation when it seems most appropriate? Why?

What is the tradition in your parish concerning the art used in the worship space?

It has been said that all true art is incarnational. What is your response?

CONSIDER

What are the traditions in your parish concerning liturgical music and congregational singing? What do these traditions say about the importance of music and singing in the liturgy?

What do you consider the most important reasons for having congregational singing? Why? What do you consider the least important reasons for congregational singing? Why?

What do you consider the most important requirements for liturgical music? Why?

P**R**AYER
p**R**EPARATION
pr**A**CTICE
pra**Y**ER

What place does music, and especially singing, have in your life? Why? What are some of your favorite pieces of music? What do you like about them? What place does music, and especially singing, have in your faith life as a Catholic Christian? Why?

What are some occasions when you have been especially moved by congregational singing? What made these occasions so memorable?

When have you felt that the music was inappropriate to the situation? Why? How can you avoid choosing music that, when it is used in the liturgy, may seem unsuitable?

What can you do, as a member of the assembly, to affirm the importance of music in liturgy?

What can you do, as a presider, to affirm the importance of music in liturgy?

What difference does it make if parishes copy music without permission? How is this a matter of justice? What is the policy at your parish concerning the copying of music? How does that affect your ministry as presider?

tasteful music; it must be imbued with a sense of the sacred. It needs to be appropriate to the community, the liturgy and the rite.

If music, and especially the singing of the assembly, are to become integral to being Catholic, then such singing should be with us wherever we go. We might consider singing at home for table graces, morning and night prayers, as a family activity, when traveling in the car. We might sing at meetings for opening or closing prayer; during retreats, days of recollection and other events; when bringing communion to the homebound; in the classroom as prayer, activity, dance, teaching aid or recreation.

Choosing Music for Liturgy. Since music is so important to the liturgy, we need to give serious thought to how it will speak to those celebrating the liturgy. If congregational singing is an integral part of liturgy, if music is the norm, and if the primary minister of music is the assembly, then including music in our worship service is as important as any other aspect of the liturgy. And that has an impact upon what we do as presiders.

Obviously, the music situation varies greatly from one faith community to another. In some communities, the liturgical director or music minister, taking into account all the particulars of the liturgy, will make the decisions concerning liturgical music. This includes choice of music and musicians; providing for worship aids, hymn boards or overhead projection; financial compensation of musicians; arrangement of worship space; and whatever else may be involved.

In other communities or for other liturgies, the presider may be responsible for some or all aspects of music for the liturgy. This could include choice of music; placement of music within the liturgy; contacting cantors, choir members and instrumentalists; overseeing payment of musicians; providing words and/or music for the assembly.

Choosing music for liturgy goes far beyond picking out an assortment of favorite hymns or psalms. Each musical element of the liturgy must be chosen carefully on its own merits and then evaluated on its place within that liturgy. These decisions will be affected by the availability of music and text for the assembly. We need to know what hymnals, booklets or song sheets are available or whether worship aids (liturgy programs for the assembly that contain some or all of the music) can be assembled. If people will not have music in hand or otherwise available, choices are limited to music that can be sung from memory or responsorial music done with a cantor.

As we consider individual musical selections, we look first at the music itself, making certain that it is appropriate musically (the tune, rhythm, tempo are all appropriate for the situation); that it is generally singable; that it will work in this particular situation with this type of accompaniment, this cantor, in this worship space, with this sound system, this assembly, at this time.

Looking at the text we ascertain that it is theologically sound, that it blends with the Scripture readings or the liturgical season, that it is communal rather than private in its praise, thanksgiving or lament, that it is appropriate to the community, to this particular liturgy, and to the ritual taking place during the singing.

Finally, we look at how each music selection fits into the liturgy, assuring a smooth flow from each element of the liturgy to the next.

A liturgical celebration can have no more solemn or pleasing feature than the whole assembly's expressing its faith and devotion in song. (Sacred Music, #16)

A liturgical service takes on a nobler aspect when the rites are celebrated with singing, the ministers of each rank take their parts in them, and the congregation actively participates.... It achieves a closer union of hearts through the union of voices. It raises the mind more readily to heavenly realities through the splendor of the rites. It makes the whole celebration a more striking symbol of the celebration to come in the heavenly Jerusalem. (Sacred Music, #5)

Among the many signs and symbols used by the Church to celebrate its faith, music is of preeminent importance. As sacred song united to words it forms a necessary or integral part of its solemn liturgy (cf. CSL 112). Yet the function of music is ministerial; it must serve and never dominate. Music should assist the assembled believers to express and share the gift of faith that is within them and to nourish and strengthen their interior commitment of faith. It should heighten the texts so that they speak more fully and more effectively. The quality of joy and enthusiasm which music adds to community worship cannot be gained in any other way. It imparts a sense of unity to the congregation and sets the appropriate tone for a particular celebration. (Music in Catholic Worship, #23)

Likewise, to ensure that composers and publishers receive just compensation for their work, those engaged in parish music programs and those responsible for budgets must often be reminded that it is illegal and immoral to reproduce by any means copyrighted texts and music without written permission of the copyright owner. The fact that these duplicated materials are not for sale but for private use does not alter the legal or moral situation of copying without permission (BCLN, April, 1969). (Music in Catholic Worship, #78)

Since most music in the liturgy, with the exception of the responsorial psalm, accompanies a ritual action, it is important that the music be appropriate to that ritual action.

An important point to remember is that not all music is liturgical, nor is all liturgical music appropriate anywhere in the liturgy.

Finally, unless the hymn is unusually long or there are extenuating circumstances, singing all verses should always be seriously considered. Otherwise, it is like stopping halfway through the recitation of the creed. Many hymn texts can be used as wonderful prayers, even without music. Some even began as prayers before they were set to music. Seeing a hymn text as a prayer often uncovers an integrity that is lost when only a part of it is sung.

A Matter of Justice. A Christian community has a duty to act honorably; the presider has a double duty as model to the community. Therefore, in justice to composers, writers and music publishers, we respect and obey the copyright laws.

Permission to copy music and/or words can be obtained from the publishers. Most publishers have an established procedure through which permission to reprint can be obtained. Many publishers will grant reprint permission to a parish or organization for a period of time, such as a year, with payment of a reasonable fee.

A presider should check with the parish administrator, the music director or the liturgical musician to learn what arrangements the parish has made with music publishers. Copying illegally "for a good cause" or "for the Church" does not make it right!

Practical Considerations. A lay presider may be presiding at a service not held in the parish church or chapel. This might be a vigil service or funeral in a mortuary, or a Word-Communion service in a nursing home or Morning Prayer in a school cafeteria. Some of these buildings may have a resident instrument, such as a piano or organ, which needs to be evaluated before the service. The parish liturgist or music director can be consulted in evaluating the resident instrument and planning the liturgy.

Some institutions have a tradition of good music and offer fine instruments for use at liturgy; others are notorious for having impoverished instruments. Should the institutional instrument be unsatisfactory, other options include using one or more guitars, flutes or strings, a synthesizer or other portable instruments for both accompaniment and/or solo work.

Many experienced cantors work quite well without accompaniment. However, when the congregational singing is unaccompanied the music should be chosen with this in mind, as some vocal music is quite dependent upon the accompaniment.

▶ *"I'm not a betting person, but if I were, I'd bet that more people leave church singing the music of the liturgy than quoting the sermon! It's the music that's the take-home theology of worship."*

▶ *"Every time I hear the Taize 'Jesus, Remember Me' I am transported back to the Good Friday liturgy; I can still picture the people approaching the cross while singing 'Jesus, Remember Me.' I don't think I'll ever forget that experience."*

▶ *"I always feel closer to God in silence and in music. It seems that it's only in silence that I can hear God—my life is so noisy and hectic! But singing is the most powerful form of my prayer. Whether I'm cantor, choir member or member of the assembly, those words become mine—my praise of God, my lament, my outpouring of doubt and faith and love and promise."*

▶ *"I think it's fascinating that Gregorian chant is making a comeback—not only in church music but even in the popular arena. Does that indicate something about the basic human need for spirituality?"*

▶ *"I often play the popular or contemporary religious music at home or in my car. When I think about the texts, I can see why many of them are not suitable for community worship or for accompanying ritual. But I still like them—and include them in my private devotions."*

▶ *"We have a presider who always sings exactly two verses of a hymn. In many hymns to the Trinity when we quit after the first two verses we never get to sing about the Holy Spirit."*

Time

Christians have a complex relationship with time. We look back in time to remember and memorialize the past; we focus on the future and proclaim God's reign; yet we are firmly committed to today, to this world, to the present. And when we gather to celebrate liturgy we telescope all of time—past, future, present—into now!

Time is a creation of, and a gift from, God. To sanctify time we dedicate Sunday to God; we proclaim the holiness of each passing day in the Liturgy of the Hours, especially Morning and Evening Prayer; we recognize the holiness of the changing seasons in our celebration of the liturgical year.

Even more important now in our efficiency-obsessed culture, is that we are willing to come together to waste time. We gather for liturgy and no product results from our efforts except the praise of God! We "waste" time in prayer, song, silence and presence to God and to each other. We gather in a place set apart from our daily world, set apart for worship, even if it is set apart only for this occasion. We gather at a time set apart—a time set "out of time."

So, what does this mean for the presider? To preside effectively we must recognize that there are two kinds of time: **chronos** time and **kairos** time. Both Greek words are used in the New Testament to describe time.

Chronos, the root of the words *chronometer* and *chronology*, refers to time as measured by a clock. *Chronos* time is impartial; it counts every second, minute and hour. *Chronos* time dominates most of our life, determining whether we are "early" or "late." It governs deadlines, appointments and alarm clocks. When we have time to "fill" or "kill," that is *chronos* time.

The other kind of time is *kairos* time, the passage of seconds, minutes and hours when we are not aware of their passing; it is the passage of time when we are removed from time and from ourselves. *Kairos* time marks our total involvement in that which is other, removing us from

CONSIDER

When are you in *chronos* time in your life? When are you most under its pressure?

How do you deal with the pressures of *chronos* time?

How might your experience of *chronos* time influence your presiding?

When do you experience *kairos* time? What are you doing?

Do you usually experience *kairos* time alone? With others? With whom do you experience it?

When do you experience *kairos* time in liturgy? In private prayer?

How might your experience of *kairos* time influence your presiding?

chronos time; it is the time of insight, imagination, daydreaming. *Kairos* time is creative, whether in areas usually considered the creative arts or in our job, profession, hobby; it is the time spent in intimacy with a dear friend or in cherishing the comfortable closeness of a soulmate or in the rapture of sexual intimacy. *Kairos* time is mountaintop time; ideally it is the time spent in a loving, intimate, wholly absorbing relationship with God.

Kairos time, according to many of the saints and mystics, is the kind of loving and intimate relationship we were created to have with our God. By means of our liturgies and the feasts and seasons of the liturgical year the Church tries to alert us to *kairos* time.

A presider needs to be concerned about both kinds of time. *Chronos* time is the reality of life and so a presider plans carefully the length of the entire service. This includes measuring the length of the sermon and considering carefully the time needed for each of the elements of the liturgy: procession, hymns, prayers, various movements, Scripture readings and so on. The presider needs to devote conscious thought to the time aspect of the service, concluding this consideration of *chronos* time by starting the liturgy at the time scheduled.

But once the liturgy begins we enter into *kairos* time. Celebrating liturgy is in *kairos* time, God's time, the time of loving, the time spent with friends. In liturgy we step out of the daily realm of the stopwatch, the time clock and the calendar; we enter into time without time, grace-filled time, the time of revelation and inspiration and intuition, the time of timeless eternity. In *kairos* time we encounter the Divine; in *kairos* time we experience God's being and we simply "are."

▶ *"Like so many people these days, I'm always in a hurry. I don't have time to pray—or else I just can't settle myself enough to pray. But then I signed up for the 3:00 to 4:00 a.m. shift at the twenty-four-hour monthly prayer service at our parish. There, in the quiet of the chapel, with no distractions, and certainly nowhere else to be, I pray!"*

Liturgical Silence

Silence can be poignant, respectful, fearful, inspiring, embarrassing, solemn, uncomfortable, anticipatory, transforming, unifying, moving. Silence can be meaningless or it can mean everything.

We are moved to silence when we contemplate the mysteries of life or face the mysteries of death, when we contemplate the vastness and beauty of creation, when we remember nothing or everything, when we hope or envision or dream, when we sense the holy.

These times occur in various forms: it may be a spectacular sunrise or sunset or the first sight and touch of our newborn child or grandchild; it may be hearing words of forgiveness or witnessing a fly-by in the "missing man" formation; it may be a scene of cooperation among individuals, peoples, nations; it may be the moments following lovemaking; it may be the changing of the guard at Arlington National Cemetery.

Silence is essential to liturgy. We need silence and contemplation to prepare for liturgy; we need liturgy to reinforce our silence and contemplation. Each is necessary for the other, because silence and

CONSIDER

When do you experience silence in your life? How do you feel about it? Why?

What are some of your memorable experiences of silence? What made them memorable?

Do you experience enough silence in your life? Too much silence? Why or why not?

When do you experience silence in liturgy? How do you feel about it? Why?

liturgy complement one another.

In liturgy, we are silent in the presence of the holy, in respect for what has been read, in contemplation of what has been said, in awe of life's paradoxes, in our self-awareness, in response to the magnificence of our loving God, in contemplation of the eternal now, in respect for the Christ within each of us, in response to the workings of the Holy Spirit.

Only in silence can we hear that most mysterious sound of our own heartbeat and confront our own existence. Such moments of silence can indeed be moments of grace.

Liturgical Movement

CONSIDER

What is the tradition in your faith community concerning liturgical dance or movement?

What is your personal reaction to liturgical dance? Why?

Keeping in mind that sacred dance is mentioned numerous times in Scripture, how do you see it fitting into liturgy?

When have you been inspired or uplifted by liturgical movement? Why?

We are embodied beings. We move, we gesture, we communicate using our bodies; at liturgy the liturgical dancer gathers up all those prayer-responses that we cannot, or choose not to, put into physical expression.

Liturgical movement, or dance, is our worship-prayer to the Choreographer of Galaxies, the God Enfleshed, the Ultimate Reality, the Cosmic Dancer; it is the fitting praise of the God of beauty and grace and energy.

Liturgical movement, as distinguished from performance, weaves together the pieces of liturgy, integrating all the other liturgical ministries; it is a mighty means of communication and the physical expression of our spirituality. Liturgical movement is art in time and space, an affirmation of our own embodiment and a most fitting response to the Incarnation.

Liturgical movement can unite the assembly in gesture; for example, to engage the whole community in the gestures of a psalm response can be a most unifying experience; it truly becomes communal prayer.

While there may be liturgies or rituals where someone carries the title of liturgical dancer, the presider needs to be aware of the importance of the graceful and grace-filled art of liturgical movement. One aspect of this is developed in the section entitled "Choreography" (page 97).

A great challenge in presiding is envisioning what our bodies and our actions communicate to others. As presiders we need to be comfortable with our bodiliness; we can often benefit from working with a liturgical dancer to become at ease with the various gestures and movements involved in presiding.

Liturgical movement or dance can be an exciting component of the assembly's worship. It is absolutely necessary, however, that the dancer understand liturgy and the role of liturgical movement in the community's worship. Just as competent skill in music is not sufficient for a liturgical musician, so too competent skills in dance are not sufficient for a liturgical dancer. Because liturgical dancers are highly visible, they need to possess many of the same qualities as presiders, especially being people of prayer. Liturgical dancing is prayer. Dancers must also be transparent, allowing the assembly's attention to go beyond the dancer to focus on the dance and the One praised in the dance.

▶ *"Before I had ever heard of liturgical dancing, I danced my prayer. Like some people might 'break into song' after an encounter with the living God, I dance! Now I have the privilege of presenting the community's prayer in sacred dance and I know that as long as my heart shall beat I shall dance!"*

Vesture

Clothes make the man—or woman! We are told that what we wear does make a difference in our social personality. We are to dress in appropriate garb if we want to be successful, intimidating, impressive, seductive or simply effective.

In addition to personal attire we may also wear readily identifiable uniforms that signify our membership in organizations, trades, professions. In other instances, our donning certain vesture indicates when we are on the job, such as when a judge wears a robe in the courtroom.

Our appearance makes statements about how we regard ourselves, what others think of us, our role in a situation and how we regard the situation. Young people often use their appearance to indicate their membership in certain groups, their independence, their protests and disdain. The young know how effective a statement personal appearance can make!

Personal appearance has an impact upon the liturgy, too; our dress expresses how we regard ourselves as members of the laity, how we regard what others think of us, how we regard our role in the liturgy and the liturgy itself.

As we make decisions about how we dress to attend liturgy, so, too, we make decisions about vesture for the cantor, lector, preacher, presider, choir. Liturgical vesture emphasizes symbolic sacred functions within the liturgy; it is not a value judgment about the person performing the function. Liturgical vesture might be compared to the uniforms people wear so that they can be readily identified, such as the outfits worn by ushers at a concert, umpires or referees at a sports event, waiters at a restaurant.

The lay presider must decide whether or not to vest. If the presider does not vest, then ordinarily the other ministers would not vest. If the presider vests, then follow-up decisions need to be made concerning other ministers of the liturgy: choir, cantor, assistants, servers, dancers, preacher. Decisions about vesture are influenced by local tradition, the type and location of the service, the assembly, and finally, by what we want to communicate by vesting or not vesting.

Important reasons favor liturgical vesture. Vesting adds dignity to a service while making it easier for others to see the presider. Vesting cloaks the personhood of the individual with the attire of the presider role and makes connections with traditions of the past. Vesting recognizes the presider as a representative of the faith community. Vesting may be practical, depending on the circumstances, and the use of liturgical vesture eliminates the possibility of the presider wearing distracting clothing. Vesting also tends to make the liturgical gestures appear more graceful.

Important reasons also favor not vesting. Not using liturgical vesture affirms the presider as a member of the assembly and diminishes perceived differences between presider and assembly. Not vesting may be more practical, again, depending upon the circumstances.

Consider these specific situations. For a group of mourners gathered around the gravesite, vesture adds dignity and solemnity to the situation and recognizes the presider as the representative of the faith community. On the parish youth camping trip, vesture may be impractical, even undesired. For a Word-Communion service held in the dining room of a nursing home, vesture may make it easier for those with poor eyesight to recognize the presider and to follow the ritual; it may also lend a touch of the formality of a time that is now only remembered. For an ecumenical service conducted by representatives of various faiths, vesture may unify or divide, depending upon the group involved.

Items of Vesture. When we attend the Sunday liturgy, the outer vestment the priest wears is called a *chasuble*. The color varies with the liturgical season or feast (see "The Liturgical Year," pages 35-37). The chasuble may be quite ornate with various designs or it may be plain. It is worn only by a priest at eucharistic liturgies.

What might vesting or not vesting symbolize to those present?

Who would vest? Who would not vest? Why?

The wearing of ritual vestment by those charged with leadership in a ritual action is an appropriate symbol of their service as well as a helpful aesthetic component of the rite (General Instruction, #297-310; Appendix to the General Instruction, #305-306). That service is a function which demands attention from the assembly and which operates in the focal area of the assembly's liturgical action. The color and form of the vestments and their difference from everyday clothing invite an appropriate attention and are part of the ritual experience essential to the festive character of a liturgical celebration (General Instruction, #308; Appendix to the General Instruction, #305-306). (Environment and Art in Catholic Worship, #93)

The *stole* is a sign of ordination. Only those who have been ordained (that is, priests and deacons) are entitled to wear the stole. A priest wears a stole around the neck; a deacon wears a stole across the upper body.

An *alb* is a long, white, sleeved, dress-type garment. A priest or deacon wears an alb under his chasuble. It is tied with a cincture—a cloth or robe belt with tassels on the ends. When a lay presider vests, then he or she wears an alb, the long white garment that became ours at baptism. The other ministers, if vesting, would also wear albs; the cantor could wear either an alb or a choir robe.

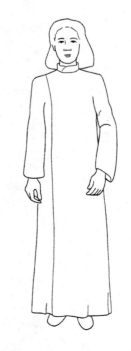

The alb is our uniform as baptized Christians. It is not a mark of hierarchy, rank or virtue; rather it indicates our membership in the Christian family. At baptism, the priest or deacon said the words, "N., you have become a new creation and have clothed yourself in Christ. Receive this baptismal garment and bring it unstained to the judgment seat of our Lord Jesus Christ, so that you may have everlasting life." The baptismal garment may have been a symbolic white garment placed over the infant or it may have been an article of clothing that the child or adult then donned. When we die and our body is brought to the church for the funeral liturgy, the presider will greet our family and friends and a pall will be placed over the casket. That pall is a symbol of our dignity as Christians and of that white baptismal garment. In between baptism and burial the alb is our baptismal garment.

The length of the alb should be chosen carefully. An alb that is too short does not accomplish the goals of vesting, while one that is too long can be a menace to movement! Be sure to practice walking and performing gestures while wearing an alb.

Some albs are fashioned of a lightweight material that is not opaque. This see-through fabric can result in the humorous or distracting appearance of the person vested. It may be necessary to give some thought to what is worn underneath the alb.

Finally, many of the albs currently hanging in sacristy closets were designed for men. Some of them look fine on some women; many women, however, when they put on the typical alb, look like a woman wearing something designed for a man. If lay presiders are to vest, a parish may want to purchase or make some albs designed for the female figure.

The basic guideline for presiding attire is comfort. This assumes, of course, that we already think of ourselves as being part of the assembly's environment. Our clothing—whether we vest or not—should reflect reverence for the presiding ministry as well as for this specific liturgy.

The presider should wear comfortable and appropriate clothes, shoes, jewelry and hairstyle. Our attire should not distract others, nor should we be unduly concerned about our appearance. Watches, especially, can be distracting; we may consult it without intending to do so, and lead the assembly or other ministers to be concerned about the time. If you will be using a lapel microphone, choose clothing that will accommodate it.

▶ *"When I was a kid I attended a parochial grade school where uniforms were required. Our teachers always told us that we were to be a credit to our school and to our uniform. Then I attended a Catholic high school. Uniforms again. And again, 'Don't do anything that would dishonor your school or your uniform!' After graduation, I entered the service. 'Don't disgrace your country or your uniform!' I realize now that no matter what our personal appearance or our work, we never are responsible just to ourselves. We are always seen as representatives of some group."*

▶ *"I volunteer as a chaplain at our annual state fair. It's a ministry of presence; we simply wander around the fairground and try to be available. It's a wonderful way to meet people and to be of service if there is need. Our uniform consists of a purple baseball cap that has 'CHAPLAIN' printed on it. That seems to suffice."*

▶ *"When I was in the army I met some fine chaplains. I noticed that the Catholic chaplain carried a very small stole folded in a pocket. Whenever he was 'on duty' as a priest he took out the stole, kissed it, then put it around his neck. When I asked him about it he said it was a sign of his ordination."*

▶ *"I preside for Word-Communion services in a nursing home. I always vest. The old dears who attend are so accustomed to being in that dining room for their meals that I try to do everything I can to remind them that we are gathered for a very special meal! I am really limited on what I can do to change the environment into one that they would recognize as a worship space. When I realized that I am part of that environment, I decided to vest. And that helps all of us!"*

▶ *"Several parishes in my city have lay preachers and each parish approaches this from a different perspective. At one church the lay preacher vests, processes in with the presider and acolytes, and remains in the sanctuary throughout the liturgy. At another church, the lay preacher does not vest, sits in the assembly, and comes forth only at sermon time. Each ritual makes statements about the liturgy and about the laity."*

Justice

CONSIDER

In what ways do your faith community's liturgies demonstrate justice and radical inclusiveness?

In what ways do your faith community's liturgies demonstrate lack of justice or inclusiveness?

How are you, personally, called to the gospel's challenge?

How is your faith community called to the gospel's challenge?

What can you do, as presider, to bring about justice in your faith community? In the world?

What is heaven like? What do we mean by the reign of God? We extend our imaginations as we search for descriptions of what lies promised before us. Yet, as we struggle with ideas and words, we can offer a comparison, for heaven and our liturgy have much in common.

The liturgy describes heaven by acting out heaven. In the symbols and rituals, the openness, hospitality and mutuality of the liturgy, we are to experience the justice and radically inclusive love that permeates the gospel. If we do not see justice prevailing within the liturgy, then where will we encounter it in the world?

Our theology says that the gospel is for all people. What do our symbols say? Our theology proclaims that we are all one family. What do our symbols say? God's love is radically inclusive; therefore, our liturgies are to be inclusive. But what do the symbols of our liturgies say?

The presider needs to be sensitive to what the symbols and rituals say, for they can outshout the most pious verbal statements. If all our visual images within our worship space are of white, Western European people—including that Middle Eastern Jewish group of Mary, Joseph, Jesus and the apostles—how welcoming is that to those of us of color?

If our scriptural language, our God-language, our prayer language, our ritual and preaching language, are all male-dominated, how welcoming is that to those of us who are women?

If our images and hymns and preaching reflect a social order based on dominance, triumphalism, sexism, racism, how welcoming is that to those of us who are marginalized or oppressed? To those of us who truly

In the earthly liturgy we take part in a foretaste of that heavenly liturgy celebrated in the holy city of Jerusalem toward which we journey as pilgrims,... (Constitution on the Sacred Liturgy, #8)

Therefore, the chosen People of God is one: "one Lord, one faith, one baptism" (Ephesians 4:5). As members, they share a common dignity from their rebirth in Christ. They have the same filial grace and the same vocation to perfection. They possess in common one salvation, one hope, and one undivided charity. Hence, there is in Christ and in the Church no inequality on the basis of race or nationality, social condition or sex, because "there is neither Jew nor Greek; there is neither slave nor freeman; there is neither male nor female. For you are all 'one' in Christ Jesus" (Galatians 3:28). (Dogmatic Constitution on the Church, #32)

While the liturgy daily builds up those who are within into a holy temple of the Lord, into a dwelling place for God in the Spirit, to the mature measure of the fullness of Christ, at the same time it marvelously strengthens their power to preach Christ, and thus shows forth the Church to those who are outside as a sign lifted up among the nations, under which the scattered children of God may be gathered together, until there is one sheepfold and one shepherd. (Constitution on the Sacred Liturgy, #2)

seek and work for peace?

If all the people involved in liturgical ministry are the beautiful people of the advertising world, then how welcoming is that to those of us who are fat, too short or too tall, have a useless limb or are otherwise less than "perfect"? What we see in liturgy not only reflects our attitudes but also reinforces those attitudes.

The liturgy is to be inclusive for there are no second-class Christians. The assembly is called to recognize the value of each and every human being, making no distinction according to wealth, prestige or education; there is to be no distinction according to age, color or sex; there is to be no distinction according to marital status, sexual orientation, ethnic background, physical capability or mental capacity.

Our liturgy is to reflect the radical mutuality and inclusiveness that announce the reign of God. Putting this into practice means the worship space is handicapped accessible; the needs of the hearing-impaired, the blind, families with young children, singles and others are recognized; the retarded, the elderly, youth, the mentally ill, the physically limited all are visible; everyone is welcomed with dignity and hospitality.

Included in our liturgies are all races, men and women, youth and children and the elderly, those of various sexual orientations, the mentally and physically challenged. In our liturgies we see people involved in liturgical ministry roles defined by their talents and abilities, not limited by bogus barriers.

▶ *"Mary and Bill were one pair of handlers for the laying on of hands at our communal penance service. However, since Mary is in a wheelchair, the only way she could put her hands on people was if they bowed down in front of her. As I leaned forward to her, I briefly saw life from a different perspective; for one profound and memorable moment, I took on her disability—and it changed me."*

▶ *"When I see the Church acting unjustly and causing people pain, then I am in pain. I grieve because we are all part of the Church, and when anyone is hurt wrongly, we are all hurt. I still love the Church! But when I see this happening, I'm determined to continue to strain toward that reign of God!"*

▶ *"Our liturgy begins and I see the priest (male, of course) presiding; I hear his prayers addressed to God the Father and God the Son; I listen to the Scriptures proclaimed to all men. And I ask myself 'Why do I, a woman, remain in this church?'"*

The Skills of Presiding

P residing places high expectations on our inner selves: knowledge and insight, reverence and hospitality, prayerfulness, love and compassion. These qualities of heart and soul are communicated mainly through our actions, so we need to acquire the practical skills involved in presiding. Through our presiding, we communicate to others what lies within.

We now consider the various gestures used in presiding; with practice, we will be able to perform them gracefully and graciously. As we work to acquire these skills, we remind ourselves: All ritual movements are learned.

> *Eternally existing Christ,*
> *only Child of only God,*
> *by your incarnation you honored forever our humanity.*
> *By your incarnation you dignified us.*
> *Help us celebrate our humanity.*
> *Increase our respect for what it means to be human.*
> *Empower us to recognize you in each other.*
> *Direct us in our worship as we—*
> *ennobled and graced humanity—*
> *gather in your name.*
> *We pray through and in and with you*
> *who lives and reigns with the Holy Spirit and the Creator,*
> *one only God, for ever and ever. Amen.*

The Primary Skill

To become effective presiders, the first skill we need to develop involves our mind and imagination: We need the ability to envision ourselves presiding.

Most of us, unless we are actors or appear often before the public, are unaccustomed to envisioning what we look like to others. Granted we may think of our appearance on the combed-hair, straightened-tie, no-slip-showing level of self-awareness. But in presiding we not only appear before the assembly, we move and read and pray and do rituals before and with the assembly. We need to become aware not only of how we look, but of what is conveyed to the assembly by what we do and how we do it. We are challenged to envision ourselves as symbols.

According to communication experts, approximately eighty-five to ninety percent of communication is nonverbal. While we may focus on words when we preside, most of what we communicate is done by actions and appearance. That's why presiders need to understand the idea of symbol and need to be aware of what they communicate while presiding.

Through our appearance we communicate reverence, respect, hospitality, love, presence and all those qualities that have already been

CONSIDER

It has been said that actions speak louder than words. How does this apply to presiding?

From your observations, what is the hardest thing for a presider to envision about presiding? Why?

When you are a member of the assembly, what do you find most distracting during a liturgy? Why? How can you, as presider, avoid distracting others?

As you begin practicing before a mirror or with others, what most surprises you about the presiding gestures and movements? Why?

discussed. All these things are communicated partly by words, but mainly by actions, posture and gesture.

As the first step listed in presider preparation was observation (see pages 4-5), so now the first skill is turning that observation on ourselves. Mentally we begin to see ourselves as presiders and envision our presiding actions.

▶ *"I took a presiding workshop, and did I learn a lot! When we were told that each of us would be videotaped presiding, a loud groan rose from the group—and then we all laughed! But the instructor explained, 'When you are presiding you will be visible to the entire assembly. Don't you want to know what you look like—and what your actions are saying to that assembly?' When I thought about it that way, I realized I really did want to see myself presiding."*

The Transparent Presider

Whether we participate in the liturgy as lector, cantor, liturgical dancer, acolyte, preacher or presider we are not intended to be the focus of the assembly's attention. When we lector well, the focus is on the reading and God's word, not on the reader. When we lead people in song well, the focus is on the sung prayer and on raising our minds and hearts and voices in song, not on the singer. When we serve well, the focus is on the ritual and the flow of the liturgy—not on the acolyte/assistant. When we dance well, the focus is on the prayer in movement, not on the dancer. When we usher well, the focus is on the service to the assembly, not on the usher. When we preach well, the focus is on the message, not on the preacher. When we preside well, the focus is on the worship experience of the congregation—not on the presider.

One of the most important qualities of a presider is transparency. To understand what that means it might be easier to point out what it does not mean. A presider's transparency does not mean a negation of our unique personality or a denial of our talents or gifts. Being transparent is not self-deprecation or false humility, an attitude that says, "I am not worthy to be a presider."

Transparency recognizes our blessedness as the People of God by uniting them in all we do as presiders. Transparency recognizes our giftedness by honoring God as the giver of those gifts. We use our gifts and talents, wherever appropriate, in our presiding ministry.

A presider's transparency allows the assembly's attention to be directed to the rituals occurring, to the word proclaimed, to the prayers prayed. A presider's transparency means that the prayer of the assembly, not the presider, is primary. A presider's transparency means the presider opens the way for the transcendent, clearing a path for the assembly's encounter with God.

While practicing the gestures and movements of presiding, we are ever mindful of our goals in presiding: to be graceful, hospitable, prayerful and transparent.

▶ *"We had a visiting presider last weekend. Since I was ushering I arrived at church early and I saw the pastor review with the visitor our parish's usual way of celebrating Mass. But that man! He made it obvious,*

What are you, as presider, most uncomfortable doing? Why?

What, as presider, are you most at ease in doing? Why?

What special understanding or familiarity do you bring to presiding?

CONSIDER

Have you ever observed a nontransparent presider? How did the presider get in the way? What was your response to the presider? To the liturgy?

How would you describe transparency? Is that going to be a challenge for you as a presider?

How does transparency affect the way you do the gestures and rituals of presiding?

What can you do to become a transparent presider?

through his overbearing ways, that it was his liturgy. As he strutted through the rituals, he demanded the assembly's attention upon himself. He was the star—and I was never able to get past him."

Liturgical Gestures

Gestures affirm the incarnation. They affirm the sanctity of our bodies. Liturgy and the sacraments glory in our existence as physical beings. The human body is our primary instrument for worship. What our body does affects our spirit.

Since our physical being is so integral to liturgy, how much more so are the movements and physical appearance of the presider. The presider is symbol to the assembly and is engaged in symbolic activity.

Becoming aware of what our movements and appearance convey to others can be challenging, but it is a skill that we can develop. The neophyte presider is often in a quandary: What do I do with my hands? How do I move? Where do I look? We can find consolation in the thought that what appears natural and relaxed to others results from work and concentration: All ritual movements are learned.

As members of the assembly and as presiders, we pray and worship with the totality of our being: standing, kneeling, lifting our hands; responding with our voices in prayer and in song; listening to reading, preaching and music; smelling the flowers, greenery and incense; encompassing in our sight all the environment, including the people who have gathered with us; acknowledging the presence of others with our touch.

We pray with our minds, hearts and spirits, and the liturgy invites our participation. Our public worship is filled with evocative symbols of our past and our future. In these liturgies we celebrate our bodiliness with gestures and ritual, firmly connecting us with life.

The various body movements and postures used in worship are called liturgical gestures. As members of the assembly we participate physically in the liturgy for our own sake, and our liturgical body language also influences the faith experience of all present. By our deliberate use of body language, we affirm our unity in ritual, belief and community; through the discipline of ritual we mold our attitudes. We make no hurried or thoughtless gestures; we favor a few simple gestures that indicate reverence, hospitality, graciousness, prayerfulness; we seek a noble simplicity in our liturgy.

Our various liturgical gestures are derived from many sources. Some date back to antiquity; others from the Middle Ages; still others are current today. The gestures of presider and assembly are integral to ritual and liturgy. They involve the entire body in prayer. They help focus our minds and hearts on the words and actions of the liturgy. Gestures provide a balance between the liturgy's verbal and symbolic elements. Gestures unify the assembly and give public testimony to our faith and our liturgy.

Our gestures are to be definite, yet not exaggerated. A sign of the cross should be recognizable as such, not suggestive of brushing away gnats. A genuflection should look like a genuflection—not like we have encountered a slippery spot on the floor tile.

When gestures are done gracefully and reverently they add to the

CONSIDER

If God can see into our hearts and souls, why bother with liturgical gestures?

Looking at the various gestures used at liturgy, what does each one symbolize to you? Which seem authentic? Do any seem contrived? If so, why?

Some Christian denominations have few gestures in their services. What are the advantages of this? The disadvantages?

How do you think a non-Christian visitor to your parish would view your liturgy? What might be his or her reaction to the liturgical gestures? How would you explain these gestures to a visitor?

What special gifts and talents do you bring to the presider role?

In an atmosphere of hospitality, posture will never be a marshaled, forced uniformity.... Those who suffer from handicaps of one sort or another, must be carefully planned for so that they can participate in the liturgy without unnecessary strain or burden. (Environment and Art in Catholic Worship, #57)

The liturgy of the Church has been rich in a tradition of ritual movement and gestures. These actions, subtly, yet really, contribute to an environment which can foster prayer or which can distract from prayer. When the gestures are done in common, they contribute to the unity of the worshiping assembly.

worship experience of the entire assembly. They draw attention not to the gesture, posture, movement or person, but to that to which the gesture, as symbol, points.

Some gestures are done by all present while others are for the presider or other ministers. The presider's gestures must support the assembly's prayer and not distract from it. For example, if a presider finds it difficult to genuflect gracefully without assistance, then that presider should use a respectful profound bow in place of the genuflection. A bow indicates respect for the holy without distracting from a congregation's prayer. The assembly should not have to hold its collective breath until the presider is once again standing!

For those gestures in which all participate, the presider models the gesture for the assembly. Through our gestures we communicate our respect for the liturgy, for the community, for God. Through our gestures we are totally involved—mind, spirit, body—in our public prayer.

 "I can't say that I became a Catholic just because of liturgical gestures. After years of being a very heady Protestant, however, I knew I had to express both my belief in God and my worship in a more complete, sacramental way. God made me as a whole human being, not just as a mind, and I feel I am called to worship with my whole body. To me, that follows from our belief in the Incarnation."

Gestures which are broad and full in both a visual and tactile sense, support the entire symbolic ritual. When the gestures are done by the presiding minister, they can either engage the entire assembly and bring them into an even greater unity, or if done poorly, they can isolate. (The Directory for Masses With Children [DMC] bases the importance of the development of gestures, postures and actions in the liturgy on the fact that liturgy, by its nature, is the activity of the entire person [see #330]). (Environment and Art in Catholic Worship, #56)

Presiding Gestures

Processing/Walking. Processing, as at the beginning and conclusion of a liturgy or at communion time, is more than just getting from one place to another. Processing moves us from *chronos* time into the *kairos* time of worship; it can be a symbol of our life's journey or pilgrimage, thereby inviting the contemplation of our own daily and yearly travels. Processing helps transform individuals into community; it communicates to the assembly that what we are about to do—or have just done—is sacred.

Processing at the start of the liturgy is also the first indication to the assembly of our preparation—or lack of it—for this liturgy. Processing, like all liturgical gestures, is to be done slowly and reverently. The presider needs to practice processing with the other liturgical ministers, giving special attention to reverencing the altar in a graceful fashion. Combining processing with bowing (discussed below), coordinates both entrance and exit.

All those in the procession reverence the altar, both when beginning the liturgy and also just before the recessional. One way to do this is to wait until everyone in the procession has arrived at the foot of the altar, then have all make a profound bow together. If the processional contingent is too large for all to reverence the altar together, reverencing the altar can be done in pairs or small groups who then move on to leave room for the following group.

Similarly, before the recessional the liturgical ministers move to the foot of the altar; when everyone is ready, all make a profound bow, turn and leave at a reverent pace.

CONSIDER

What does processing symbolize for you?

Have you ever been impressed by watching a procession? By participating in a procession? How and why?

What does the communion procession mean to you?

How can you process as a presider so as to invite others to contemplate life as a journey or pilgrimage?

 "Hurry, hurry, hurry—that's me! But when I recently attended the

blessing of a friend's home, we met in the garage and, while singing, marched very slowly around to the front of the house. That's when I realized how rarely I walk so deliberately!"

What does a bow symbolize for you? A profound bow?

How do you feel, as a member of the assembly, when a presider bows to you before a sprinkling rite or an incensing rite? Why?

Bowing. Bowing is a graceful and ancient way of showing honor and respect. In some cultures people bow to one another in recognition of the divine that resides in each of us.

Two types of bows are used in liturgy. In a regular bow we lean forward, moving the head forward and downward. With this gesture we convey respect, recognition, gratitude.

Some people incorporate a bow during the sign of peace or before receiving communion. The presider may bow to another when being handed a ritual object or book or before performing an incensing or sprinkling rite.

The other gesture is the profound bow. We perform this movement from the waist, bending forward to form an approximate right angle with our legs and upper body. This bow is more solemn than the regular bow and is used in place of genuflection in reverencing the altar. With a profound bow we acknowledge the Holy, the Limitless, the Mystery of God.

How would you welcome a good friend?

What does a presider's reading of the greeting signify to you? Why?

What does a presider's greeting without the hand gesture signify to you? Why?

What does a presider singing the greeting signify to you?

Welcoming Gesture. How do we welcome loved ones? How do we receive the child running toward us? How do we indicate acceptance, vulnerability? We communicate with open arms! Our extended and open hands speak eloquently. This is the gesture used to greet and welcome the assembly at the beginning of the liturgy. And since the focus of that gesture is the assembly, we look at the assembly, taking in the entire gathering.

Memorizing the short liturgical greeting—said or sung—enables us to do this gesture sincerely and authentically. It would be difficult to do it adequately while holding a book.

What does standing during liturgy signify to you as a member of the assembly? What does standing during liturgy signify to you as a presider?

As you observe various presiders standing, what hand position looks most natural? Most reverent? Most artificial?

What aspect of standing offers the most challenge to you as a presider-to-be? What can you do to overcome this challenge?

Standing. Standing is a posture of respect. Standing conveys dignity, honor, deference. In our culture we stand for the presentation of our flag and at the entrance and the exit of the president, court justices and other dignitaries. We stand for ovations and the singing of the Hallelujah Chorus from Handel's *Messiah* and the bride's entrance in the wedding procession.

Standing also indicates our unity with those present. We "take a stand" to show our loyalty and "Arise!" to show our readiness and alertness. We stand to receive our orders, for recognition and to be sent forth on a mission.

Thus, at liturgy we stand for the entrance procession and greeting, for the reading of the Gospel, to make our professions of faith, during the Eucharistic Prayer, to receive communion, to bless and be blessed, to be sent forth on our mission.

Standing is also an ancient and most evocative manner of professing our belief in the Resurrection. Thus we stand attentively. We do not stand with the precision of military "*Attention!*" but rather with reverence.

Practice standing in front of a mirror: with arms hanging straight down; with hands folded or clasped together; dressed in vesture. Evaluate: What looks natural? Reverent? Distracted? Respectful? Artificial? Impatient? Bored? Attentive? Stilted?

People model what they see; as presiders we model the properly reverent way for the assembly to stand.

What does sitting during liturgy signify to you as a member of the assembly? What does sitting during liturgy signify to you as a presider?

As you observe various presiders sitting, what body position looks most natural? Most reverent? Artificial? Bored?

As you observe various presiders sitting, what hand position looks most natural? Most reverent? Artificial? Impatient?

Sitting. When we are not moving or engaging in physical activity we are most aware of our body. What should we do with our hands? Where should we look? Suddenly we may feel self-conscious of our visibility as presiders.

The seated presider assumes a posture of attentive watchfulness, of receptive participation. The presider is at rest, but is listening, open, inwardly active. This takes practice and self-awareness.

For example, what do we want to communicate to the congregation when we are seated and the lector is reading or the preacher is preaching or the cantor is leading the singing? We want to communicate that we are actively listening. The ancient Hebrews understood that listening is not passive; their word for *word* is the same as their word for *action*.

So, as we listen attentively, we are seated with our back straight, both feet on floor. We refrain from toe-tapping. While we may be accustomed to crossing our legs when we are seated, this looks too casual for presiding.

Our hands may be on the chair armrests. We must take care, however, not to look as though we are about to spring forth from the chair. Our hands may be in our lap, but they are at rest—with no drumming or flexing of fingers.

While seated we refrain from leafing through the worship aid or presider book. Such activity or movement conveys to the congregation impatience, lack of concentration on the words being said, read or sung, lack of consideration for the speaker, lack of interest in what is happening.

The Orans. The posture of the *orans* is the classical attitude of prayer: standing with both arms raised to the side and extended upward, elbows bent, palms facing forward. In this open-handed posture we signify to God and to each other our readiness either to give or to receive.

What aspect of sitting offers the most challenge to you as a presider-to-be? What can you do to overcome this challenge?

What does the *orans* symbolize for you? Why?

What is your response to an ordained minister assuming the *orans* stance? What is your response to a lay minister assuming the *orans* stance? If there is any difference, why?

How do you feel about using this gesture during presiding? Why?

The *orans* is described numerous times in Scripture: "So I will bless you as long as I live;/I will lift up my hands and call on your name" (Psalm 63:4). "Lift up your hands toward the holy place, and bless the LORD" (Psalm 134:2). At the dedication of the temple, "Solomon stood before the altar of the LORD in the presence of all the assembly of Israel, and spread out his hands to heaven. He said, 'O LORD, God of Israel...'" (1 Kings 8:22, 23).

This is the presider's stance of prayer; it indicates that we are offering to God the prayers of the entire assembly. It is important to practice this stance before a mirror or with another person evaluating our effectiveness. The *orans* is distinct from either signaling "touchdown!" or the customary "hands-up!" at gunpoint. Also, if not done properly, it can be construed as a barrier the presider uses to keep others at a distance. The assembly should be spared such confusing signals.

The *orans* posture is used during prayer; therefore, the presider does not make eye contact with the assembly. The presider either looks at the written word, looks down, looks out past the assembly or has eyes closed.

Many of the presider's prayers end with the assembly's "Amen." The cue to the assembly is both aural and visual: We offer a familiar ending, such as "We ask this through our Lord Jesus Christ, your Son, who lives and reigns with you and the Holy Spirit, one God, for ever and ever." As we are praying this, we bring our hands down and together, while moving our head to look at the assembly for their "Amen."

Having an assistant often makes it easier to pray in the *orans* stance. One technique is for the presider, while facing the assembly, to open the book to the correct page, then hold the book at the desired distance and height for easiest reading. The assistant, who stands facing the presider to the side, then takes hold of the book without moving it and holds it while the presider prays. This allows the assembly to see the presider while the presider offers the assembly's prayer.

In assuming the *orans* stance we connect with our ancient past, both in Hebrew Scripture times and in the early Church. One of the earliest pictorials of the Church is found in the catacomb of Saint Priscilla in Rome, where the Church is portrayed as a woman with her arms outstretched as if in prayer. We, as presiders, are symbols of the Church at prayer.

Kneeling. The posture of kneeling has long been regarded as one of penitence, subservience, petition, adoration or piety. We kneel less during the post-Vatican II liturgy because we recognize that while we gather for worship as sinners needing forgiveness, we also gather as blessed and gifted creations of a loving God who became one of us.

Standing and sitting are now used for most of our worship, but kneeling is still used for penitential rites and reconciliation services and at other special times. Kneeling, like any other posture, should be done reverently. The posture calls for a straight back forming a straight line down to our knees.

It is especially important that the presider present an acceptable model for the assembly when kneeling. Presiders who have difficulty kneeling should sit or stand.

Genuflecting. Genuflecting has been part of our tradition since feudal times. It is often replaced by bowing in today's liturgy. For a simple genuflection, kneel briefly on the right knee. A "double" genuflection (kneeling briefly on both knees) is used when the Blessed Sacrament is exposed, as during a service of Forty Hours or other times of eucharistic adoration.

What does kneeling symbolize for you? What does standing symbolize for you? How does our posture in liturgy reflect our theology?

Does kneeling have a place in your private prayer and devotions? Why?

If we believe that Christ is present in the assembly then how do we reflect that belief with our posture?

At a liturgy not held in a church or chapel, how would you determine appropriate postures for the assembly? For yourself as presider?

Do you regard genuflection as a tradition of Catholicism or as a tradition of the Middle Ages? Why?

How do you feel about genuflecting? About replacing genuflecting with bowing? Why?

Is the Sign of the Cross the symbol of our faith? If not, what is it? Why?

Some non-Catholic Christians maintain that the Sign of the Cross belongs to all Christians and all should feel free to use it. What is your response?

CONSIDER

How do you respond to someone who does not look at you during a conversation? Why?

As you observe presiders, what is most noticeable about where they look at various times during the liturgy? What good models have you observed? What are you learning from less effective presiders?

When you are nervous about presiding, what might your facial expressions communicate?

As you observe other presiders what adjectives come to mind: happy? haughty? bored? loving? distracted? present? accepting? arrogant? suffering?

What do you think will be the most difficult aspect of this for you? Why?

What specific skills do you bring to presiding?

Sign of the Cross. The sign of our faith is the Sign of the Cross. When the rites were revised following the Second Vatican Council, one major change was a simplification of many repeated rituals. This allowed a greater focus on what remained. The numerous repetitions of the Sign of the Cross were replaced with a meaningful, reverent gesture at the beginning and end of the liturgy. As presiders we model this gesture for the assembly as a sign of our faith! It indicates our faithfulness to the liturgy, the assembly and our God.

According to instructions in the rites, when lay presiders bless the assembly we do not make the Sign of the Cross over the assembly; that is reserved for the ordained. Instead, we sign ourselves with the members of the assembly.

Focal Points

Where does the presider look while performing these gestures or assuming these positions? Two guidelines help us answer that question.

The first guideline deals with those situations when the focus of the liturgy is another person (or persons). In these instances the presider looks at that person: the lector, the cantor, the preacher. When the presider looks at whoever is the focus of the liturgy the assembly focuses on that person also.

Sometimes the placement of furniture makes this difficult or awkward. It may only be possible to turn slightly toward the reader/speaker. If we have any input into the arrangement of furniture in the liturgical space, we should remember to allow for watching whomever is the liturgical focus at any time.

If it is not possible or comfortable to look at the minister, what then? Usually, we will look downward or out beyond the assembly or slightly above the assembly.

Even if the presider cannot look at the individual who is ministering, the presider still is an example to the assembly: to look through the presider's book during the singing of the psalm communicates lack of respect for the cantor and congregation's part in the liturgy; to fidget during the lector's reading communicates lack of respect for both the Scripture and the other member of our faith community, while the movement draws attention to the presider rather than the lector.

The presider may also listen with eyes closed, but only if the posture conveys an attitude of active listening. The assembly should be confident that the presider is not sleeping!

Our second guideline concerns personal encounters and exchanges, such as the greeting and the Sign of Peace. During the greeting the presider looks at the assembly. Similarly, when exchanging the Sign of Peace, we look at the person we are greeting. There certainly is a lack of sincerity or commitment in our action if, as we are extending to our neighbor the peace of Christ, we are looking at our shoes or glancing at people three pews back.

If an assistant hands us a book or ritual item, we look at that person when we receive it. This helps us be present to what we are doing and to the liturgy itself. If we are serving as a eucharistic minister, when we hold up the bread or the cup and announce the presence of Christ, we look at the person who is communing.

No matter where we focus our attention, our facial expression should reflect the presider qualities mentioned before; ideally, our face would say to the assembly: "I am here, now! And I am so pleased to be with you at our liturgy!"

A discussion of where to focus our attention and our eyes when we are reading or praying is presented on pages 77-79.

▶ *"My son Michael and I were attending liturgy at my parents' church. Michael seemed intrigued by the statue of the Blessed Mother holding the Holy Infant. As we were leaving, he pointed to the statue. 'Why does the mother have that angry look on her face? And why isn't she looking at the baby—doesn't she like him?'"*

Incensing

The use of incense in religious rituals predates written history. Incense was an integral part of the worship of biblical Israel and has long been associated with worship in our Catholic tradition. Several liturgies offer the opportunity to perform an incensing rite.

Consider Psalm 141:2: "Let my prayer be counted as incense before you,/and the lifting up of my hands as an evening sacrifice." Here we have an example of both the use of incense and the lifting up of our hands in supplication, as in the *orans* posture.

Incensing a person or an object recognizes the sacredness that exists there. Usually in an incensing rite the presider incenses the altar, then the ambo, then the assembly. The presider approaches each object/person, bows, incenses, then bows again before moving to the next place.

A considerate presider does not make the congregation guess about the incensing procedure. Moving from section to section of the assembly, the presider approaches people from the front so they can see the presider's bow and respond if they wish.

The ritual container used for the incensing rite, like everything else involved in liturgy, is symbolic. The traditional thurible is usually made of silver or gold-colored metal and hangs on a chain; typically it is swung three times in any single direction.

CONSIDER

What does the incensing ritual mean to you? Why?

What is the tradition in your parish concerning the use of the incensing rite? How is it usually done? Who does it?

What do you like about the incensing ritual? Dislike?

How would you like to do the incensing ritual? What do you need to practice?

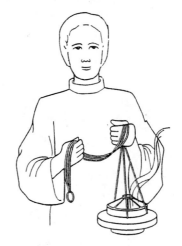

The presider can also carry an incense bowl of metal or pottery. Various movements can be made with the incense bowl during the rite. The presider might make large, sweeping circles before the persons/object, make a large sign of the cross or use another symbolic motion.

However the rite is done, whether the presider or assistant or liturgical dancer does the incensing, it needs to be well-planned; the course through the assembly needs to be decided in advance. To do it gracefully, we need to practice.

▶ *"Our parish Evening Prayer always includes an incensing rite. As presider, I usually do the incensing—unless we have a liturgical dancer. I first incense the altar—the table of the Lord; then the ambo—where the word of God is read. But when I incense the people I begin blinking back tears! I'm not blessing them—rather, I have the privilege of honoring the blessedness that already exists within each and every one of them!"*

Sprinkling Rite

The sprinkling rite is another ritual that can be used in a number of liturgies; the varied symbolism of water makes it a powerful element of ritual. We bless water and we bless with water, changing the details of the rite to fit the occasion.

Traditionally a metal sprinkler was used for the rite; often today an evergreen branch or another natural object is used for the sprinkling. As with all items used in liturgy, the container chosen for the water should be of suitable quality and appearance.

If the rite involves all the people, we approach them from the front so they know that the rite is taking place. An assistant may help with the rite by carrying the water.

Blessing

"AaaaaaAAH CHOOOOOOOO!"

"God bless you!"

How easily we bless a sneezer—someone we might not even know! We may be seated on a bus or in line at a ticket window when the person next to us sneezes, and, without a moment's hesitation, we bless that person!

CONSIDER

How would you describe the difference between blessing a person and praying for that person?

How do you regard the priest's blessing at the end of a liturgy? How do you regard the lay presider's blessing at the end of a liturgy? Is there a difference in your reaction? Why or why not?

Does your faith community consider themselves blessers? Why or why not?

What does the assembly's joining in the blessing by extending their hands over the person or object to be blessed symbolize for you?

When have you blessed another person? How did it feel?

How do you feel about doing blessing rituals?

The celebration of blessings holds a privileged place among all the sacramentals created by the Church for the pastoral benefit of the people of God. As a liturgical action, the celebration leads the faithful to praise God and prepares them for the principal effect of the sacraments. By celebrating a blessing the faithful can also sanctify various situations and events in their lives. In ordering the reform of sacramentals, Vatican Council II decreed that in their celebration special attention should be given to the full, conscious, and active participation of the faithful. (Book of Blessings, Decree)

Although blessing one another has been part of our tradition since scriptural times, at some point in our religious history we laity turned from this rich heritage, relinquishing the privilege of blessing to the ordained. Yet blessing one another is simply asking God's favor upon that individual. Scripture tells of many occasions when parents blessed their children or friends blessed one another; the members of the early Church bestowed blessing upon each other. To say to a friend, "I'll pray for you" means that we intend to ask God's grace upon that individual—why do we not bless that person?

If we are what we claim to be, a sacramental people, then the rituals and blessings of our faith are too important to our lives to be confined to church liturgies. If we are what the Second Vatican Council proclaimed us to be, then we recognize the sacramentality of everyday life.

An incarnational spirituality is based upon the unveiling of God's presence in the ordinary. Our worship begins by celebrating this divine presence in our world and in each other.

Now, as we begin presiding, we reclaim these beautiful blessing rituals in all their uplifting and affirming grandeur—not only for us as presiders but for all the baptized. Truly, our vocation is one of blessing! As People of God we have a right and a duty to bless each other and our universe.

Blessing is not something we do to people, for people themselves are blessings. Rather, in a blessing ritual, we give praise and thanks to God both for the person being blessed and for ourselves as we ask God's grace upon us.

As lay presiders, we bless both people and things. Many rites close with a blessing; other rites include blessing, anointing and incensing rituals. The lay presider may be involved in Ash Wednesday rituals, the laying on of hands, the blessing of a home or a burial site, the blessing of water or oil to be used in ritual.

When blessing a person or an object, we can invite all present to join us in the blessing by extending their hand or hands out and over the person or object to be blessed. This allows for more participation of the assembly and affirms all of us in our own blessedness.

At present, the rites usually specify that ordained presiders make the sign of the cross over the assembly or the object or others, while lay presiders make the Sign of the Cross on themselves.

▶ *"The unusual and noisy assemblage formed in front of the university chapel and extended into the street. There, in the middle of a campus renowned for its science and skepticism, people stood holding, cradling, tethering their pets, awaiting the annual Blessing of Animals. It was October 4, the feast of St. Francis."*

▶ *"I've often noticed that a priest, while distributing communion, will make the Sign of the Cross on the forehead of an infant or a small child; I've also noticed how rarely a lay eucharistic minister does likewise."*

▶ *"There certainly is a broad spectrum of belief among Catholics concerning blessing! As a lay presider, I had been invited to plan and preside for the blessing of a beautiful new house. The ceremony included singing and instrumental music, the blessing of water by all present and then a sprinkling rite by the owners and guests. As I was preparing the worship aid in the parish center a man entered carrying two candles. 'Is a priest available?' he asked. 'I'd like these candles blessed.'"*

CONSIDER

What does anointing symbolize for you?

How does anointing someone who is ill compare to praying for that person?

How important is the touch of loved ones in your life?

What is the effect upon the assembly at an anointing liturgy? How does such a liturgy affect you?

What does anointing symbolize about the body?

Have you, or someone close to you, ever been anointed? What were your reactions?

How do you feel about anointing someone? Why?

Anointing and Laying on of Hands

The word *Christ* means "anointed one." As followers of Christ we are anointed—and we also anoint. Although the administration of the Sacrament of Anointing is reserved for the ordained, the nonordained may perform a lay anointing. Anointing is another way of blessing, of physically indicating our heart prayers, of honoring the anointed. Often a laying on of hands is part of an anointing, although each ritual may be performed alone.

Reasons for an anointing and/or laying on of hands tend to fall into two main categories: (1) as a prayer for physical and mental health, healing of relationships, wholeness of body, preparation for death; (2) as a commissioning or a sign of recognition and honor. Examples of both kinds of anointing are found in Scripture as well as in tradition.

Healing. The Sacrament of Anointing has its roots in the healing rituals and treatments of the Hebrew Scriptures, where oil, valued for food and cooking and lighting, was also used as a balm and as medicine. Blessed oil was used in the early Church in healing rituals that recognized the sanctity of the body and the power of human touch and prayer.

One certainly does not need to be at the point of death to benefit from being anointed! Yet, somehow anointing became reserved as an Extreme Unction, a ritual to be performed only at the time of death. Following the Second Vatican Council, anointing has been restored to its rightful place in our Catholic treasury of helps for life. We now have anointing services for the aged and the ill. And we have reclaimed our right to anoint one another and pray for one another in a laying on of hands ritual.

The lay presider may be called upon to lead a healing service within the community or may do lay anointings during visits of the ill and aged at home or in institutions. There are no required prayers for such services. It might begin with a simple reminder that we are always in the presence of God. This could be followed by an appropriate Scripture reading and some words about healing, anointing, the laying on of hands or our belief in the might of prayer.

It is not necessary to have blessed oil for the anointing. However, since the prayers of an assembly, even a small one, are the prayers of the Church, it is desirable to have the group bless the oil to be used. The presider may do the blessing of the oil, with everyone present extending hands over the container. Or, the presider may bless the oil and then pass the container so that everyone present may add a personal blessing. Usually olive oil is used, with fragrance added if desired. The light, lingering smell of aromatic oil reminds the one anointed of the prayers of the Church.

Exactly how the anointing is accomplished is determined by our consideration for the one anointed and our awareness of the power of symbol. The actual touching during the anointing is often done by the anointer dipping a thumb in the blessed oil and then making the sign of the cross on the person, but this is not required. Our touch may be light or vigorous, but the touch needs to be felt by the one anointed, for touch is the most fundamental sense.

We may choose to anoint the person's palms and/or forehead, feet, senses (eyes, ears, mouth, nose, hands). We might anoint the person's hands with our hands, spreading the oil over all the fingers. We might anoint the person's particular area of disease or pain.

The anointing may be done in silence or with an appropriate prayer:

- "May Christ, the Divine Physician, bring you health of body and peace of mind and spirit."
- "Through this blessed oil may you be restored to wholeness and health."
- "Creator, Savior, Sanctifier, bless (Name)."

As individuals complete the anointing they may keep their hands upon the person's shoulders or head or body as others anoint. This keeps the person being anointed aware of their presence and prayers. This laying-on-of-hands in the midst of a concerned and praying community is tremendously powerful and affirms our faith in God and in prayer.

An anointing service could be held for a family member or friend who is ill, a person facing surgery, chemotherapy, radiation treatments, a person going through a difficult emotional time, a person fighting depression or other form of mental illness, an elderly friend.

Through the touch of anointing we, though wounded ourselves, help bring healing to others. Through the physical contact of anointing we convey to others our prayers for their healing and peace and our recognition of the sacredness of each of us.

Commissioning. Anointing is also a way to recognize an individual's accomplishments, the attainment of a goal, the beginning of a new venture, the presence of the Holy Spirit. A laying on of hands may also be included in the anointing ritual.

When we were baptized, we were anointed; when we were confirmed, we were anointed. When men are ordained as priests and deacons, they are anointed. And so we continue to anoint to empower a person's calling, affirm another's vocation or to recall the ministry that we all have through our baptism into the priesthood of Christ.

An anointing service could be held for one leaving for college, a new job, the military, the Peace Corps; in a prayer group with all anointing each other; as a sign of commissioning to conclude a ministry day; as a commissioning to proclaim the gospel; as a final farewell to one who is dying; as a closing ritual for a retreat or Bible study course; in recognition of the presence of the Holy Spirit; as a symbol of unity.

Those present may bless the oil and the anointing itself may be done however seems most appropriate. Those gathered might pray for vigor and fortitude, for courage, for wisdom or in gratitude to God for the gift of the person anointed.

Anointing, like life, is messy! The oil stays on our body, soaks into our skin, becomes part of us, affirming our own messy blessedness.

▶ *"When our daughter was expecting our first grandchild there were complications of her pregnancy. We were very worried! My husband and I gathered the rest of the family and we prayed over our daughter and her unborn baby. It was an overwhelmingly powerful experience!*

Have you ever been anointed in a commissioning rite? What were your reactions?

What does a commissioning anointing symbolize for you?

What do you see as the benefits of such a commissioning anointing? Any drawbacks?

How would you feel about presiding at a commissioning anointing? Why?

Gathered together, her husband, we her parents, and her brothers and sisters anointed her. After all, who could pray more sincerely, more deeply than we?"

▶ *"The day before my surgery my friends gathered and anointed me. We prayed over the small dish of olive oil, asking God's blessing. Then they anointed me—my forehead and my hands—and prayed for a complete and speedy recovery. I went into surgery feeling calm and blessed!"*

▶ *"Our retreat concluded with an anointing ritual. The presider anointed four people by signing both hands of the person and then enclosing them in his own as he prayed silently. Those four then went to the assembly and anointed others in the same manner; these, in turn, anointed the persons next to them. I watched hands being held lovingly and long, as spouses anointed each other, parents and children anointed one another, friends anointed friends. As the ritual slowly moved throughout the assembly tears flowed freely! Finally, the last person in the assembly to be anointed then anointed the presider."*

Singing

At one time all presiders sang. Back in the days of the "High Mass" the priest was required to sing or chant certain parts of the liturgy, and so it was done. While some of these men were gifted musically, most were not. They did, however, get help from liturgical musicians; they practiced and learned the parts they were to sing; they sang with the voices God gave them. Admittedly, some singing was quite distracting to the congregation (and probably humbling to the singer); however, mostly it was both accepted and acceptable.

During the transition times following the Council, liturgical texts were revised and revised again. The numerous changes in these texts made it difficult for the musically limited to learn to sing them, resulting in a declining number of singing presiders.

The irony is that this occurred during the time when congregational singing was increasing. As the assembly gradually assumed its musical role as vocal participant in the liturgy, the presiders relinquished theirs! And yet, the reasons for the assembly's singing remain valid for the presider: singing heightens the texts, giving them solemnity and prominence; singing together is unifying and enjoyable; singing is the norm; the essence of the liturgical rite is musical.

Certainly the presider, as model for the assembly, joins with the assembly in singing the hymns and responsorial refrains. Even when a cantor is present, parts of some liturgies are more appropriately sung by the presider and are so marked in the rite books. The opening greeting, the dialogues with the assembly, the blessings—these are truly enhanced when sung.

Almost anyone can learn to sing well enough to be a singing presider. Just as those priests years ago were able to learn their parts, so, too, can we. With assistance from a liturgical musician or a voice coach, we can learn melodies, improve our ability to stay on pitch and develop an acceptable sense of rhythm.

Some people are self-conscious about singing in public, reflecting a

PRAYER
PR**E**PARATION
PR**A**CTICE
PRA**Y**ER

belief that if we are not gifted with an exceptional voice then we should be quiet. Such an attitude needs to be examined carefully. Our voice is a gift from God to be used for the greater glory of God. If we choose not to sing, we need to consider whether it is personal pride that prevents our singing. Are we not denigrating the works of creation by our refusal to sing? What are we communicating to the assembly with our silence?

The importance of our singing becomes obvious when we remember that presiders who sing are models for the assembly's participation. By our singing we validate and facilitate the assembly's singing.

At each and every liturgy, let *all* voices join together as do the heavenly choirs in singing the praises of God!

Silence

Silence is an integral and necessary part of liturgy. Silence may serve as a transition from one ritual element to another. Or silence may be the only appropriate response to what has been experienced.

For an assembly, communal silence can be a profound and unifying ritual. The large gathering, silent out of respect or awe, speaks most eloquently with but a single voice.

The presider must be careful to allow the assembly to enter into silence. That period of time can be a moment of grace, for all present. Making possible the enjoyment of silence is another skill that the presider needs to acquire.

In the rite books the directions often include the words: "a period of silence," following, for example, the invitation "let us pray," the readings, the homily and communion. A period of silence can also follow any moving, Spirit-filled ritual. But just how long is "a period of silence"? How does the presider know when to end the silence?

Many factors determine the appropriate length of silence within a liturgy, including the kind of service it is, the environment, the age of the assembly members, the comfort of those present, the expectations of the assembly and community tradition.

For example, at a weekend retreat people would expect longer periods of silence than at a typical parish Morning Prayer service. Similarly, the length of silence that is comfortable in a faith-sharing group meeting in a comfortable home environment may be much too long for a children's liturgy held in a school gym.

One way to determine an appropriate time for silence is to observe an experienced presider and actually count the length of silence allowed: one-thousand-one, one-thousand-two, one-thousand-three....

Another way to assess a comfortable length of silence is to listen to the assembly during that silence. Usually a sound-pattern emerges: first, there is some movement and noise as the congregation initially settles into the silence; that is followed by quiet; then, after what the assembly senses as "enough" silence, there is again movement and noise as the people indicate their readiness to continue the liturgy. A hospitable presider listens to what the assembly is saying—it is their prayer!

CONSIDER

What do you think is the place of silence or contemplation in ritual?

When have you had a profound experience of communal silence? What made it so memorable?

In your faith community is liturgical silence respected and appreciated? Why or why not?

What is your attitude toward communal silence? Why?

How would you, as presider, determine an appropriate period of silence?

To promote active participation, the people should be encouraged to take part by means of acclamations, responses, psalmody, antiphons, and songs, as well as by actions, gestures, and bearing. And at the proper times all should observe a reverent silence. (Constitution on the Sacred Liturgy, #30)

silence
silence
silence
the profound experience of communal silence
silence
silence
silence
silence
silence
silence
silence
silence

Communal silence is a fragile entity! It can be broken in several ways: by sound, movement, signals, actions of other ministers, other distractions within the worship space. When we plan the silence within a liturgy we must assure that the silence is not broken by other activities happening during that time.

▶ *"I regard the silence during the liturgy as potential moments of blessing. I need time for the music to drift into quiet, for the echoes of prayer or Scripture or preaching to fade. That's when the Holy Spirit is most active; for me, these are the moments of blessing, of transformation."*

Words

As presiders we do a lot of reading aloud. We read prayers, Scripture, sermons, stories, petitions, eulogies, proclamations, directions, explanations, announcements and any other form of the written word. Surely we need no reminders of the importance in the liturgy of these words read aloud. We now consider words and our preparation and practice for speaking these words in liturgy.

> *Word of God,*
> *enfleshed for us and our salvation,*
> *you spoke to our ancestors in parables and stories.*
> *With words, you healed bodies and transformed hearts;*
> *with words, you taught and prayed.*
> *Help us now*
> *to enter into your parables and stories*
> *in this time and place,*
> *within this faith community.*
> *You who are Word,*
> *make our proclamations come alive!*
> *Let all who hear your holy Scripture,*
> *be touched by your power and love.*
> *We ask this in your name,*
> *You who are the Word,*
> *living and reigning*
> *in union with the Creator and the Spirit,*
> *one God, for ever and ever. Amen.*

The Audience for Our Words

As we begin to prepare the words of a liturgy the first question we should ask about each item is simply, "What is this?" Each reading needs to be identified. Is it a greeting, a prayer, a Scripture reading, an announcement, a direction, an invitation, a sermon or something else?

The identification of a reading determines the audience. We address the assembly in greetings, Scripture readings, proclamations, announcements, sermons, eulogies or stories. We address God in prayers, petitions or intercessions. No matter who we are addressing, the assembly should be able to hear and understand all words said aloud. Knowing who is being addressed, however, determines for the presider both posture and focus.

Addressing the Assembly. Almost any time we, as presiders, deliver the spoken or sung word, we stand. We stand when saying or singing prayers, when reading Scripture, when addressing the assembly. If another person is reading Scripture, preaching or leading the assembly in song, then that person would usually stand, while the presider, in turn, is seated, focusing attention on the other person. Standing is a noble posture of respect, conveying both dignity and deference; the presider

CONSIDER

From your observations of presiders, lectors, preachers, cantors, what are some of the attitudes and beliefs communicated to the assembly by their stance and gestures? By their eye contact, or lack of it, with the assembly?

When have you felt that a lector was reading specifically to you? Why?

When have you felt that the presider was unaware of the assembly? Why?

Do you usually feel included in your faith community's liturgies? Why or why not?

How do you like to be greeted at a gathering by the host? How do you like to be greeted by a close friend? By your family? By a presider?

In some cultures there are situations where it is considered impolite to look directly at another person. How might this affect presiding? What is the tradition in your community?

What are some presiding situations when standing seems most appropriate? When sitting seems appropriate?

How important is eye contact when reading or speaking to an assembly?

Do the worship spaces where you will preside favor the presider making eye contact with the assembly? If there are problems, what can be done to correct them?

usually stands in reverence for God, in respect for the assembly, in respect of the sacred task of serving the assembly.

In addition to standing out of reverence or respect, there are other practical reasons for standing, such as to provide improved visibility to the assembly, to be heard better or to provide a focal point for the assembly's attention.

Exceptions include a children's liturgy, where the presider might sit among the children to tell a story or to pray, or a small gathering where it seems more hospitable to be seated among the participants. The presider's first function is as minister of hospitality.

Special considerations should be made with regard to those who have difficulty standing or walking. Certainly the ability to stand should not be a deciding factor in whether a person is qualified to preside, or to serve as lector. The inclusion in the liturgy of the physically limited is a matter of justice, compassion and love. Therefore, the community should provide for the accessibility, visibility and safety of all who serve the community in the liturgy.

Since it is customary in our society to look at the person or persons to whom we are speaking, we usually look at the assembly when addressing them, as much and as often as possible. This point should be kept in mind when tending to the physical set-up of the worship space.

Acquiring the skill to read effectively requires practice. Only through practice will we develop a comfortable pace of reading, the correct voice level for the worship space, the comfortable stance and effective eye movement for communication. What we are comfortable doing we will do well.

Two instances deserve special attention: the times when we expect a response from the assembly and the opening greeting of a liturgy.

Often during a rite the presider says a prayer with the expectation that the assembly will add an "Amen" at the appropriate time. During the prayer the presider assumes the *orans* posture, with eyes on the presider book or rite book; as the presider begins the closing words of the prayer, such as "we ask this through Christ our Lord" the hands are brought downward and together while the eyes are raised to the assembly, cuing the people to add their "Amen."

In a similar way a lector reading the intercessions will read the intercession (a prayer) with eyes on the book. Then, as each intercession concludes with a phrase such as "We pray to the Lord," the lector looks up and out at the assembly, cuing the assembly for its response.

Finally, a note about the greeting at the beginning of a liturgy. This is an especially important ritual; here the presider first verbally expresses hospitality to the assembly and initiates rapport. A presider will find it difficult to communicate a feeling of "I am so pleased to be here with you in prayer" while focusing on the rite book. Also, since the gesture of greeting is made with extended arms, either holding the book or having the book between the presider and the assembly diminish the welcoming aspect of the greeting. It is worthwhile to memorize the opening greeting. Since the greeting is usually familiar and relatively short, this is not an unrealistic goal.

Addressing God. When we pray aloud we address God. As with our other spoken words, we speak distinctly, slowly, reverently. Even though we are addressing God, we are praying in the name of the assembly and so they should be able to hear and understand their prayer.

In general, we stand. And, if our hands are free, then the custom is to assume the *orans* posture, one of the oldest prayer-postures (described on pages 63-65).

We look at the assembly while addressing that assembly, but where do we look when we are addressing God? Since we are not addressing the assembly, we ordinarily do not look at them during a prayer. When praying, we keep our eyes focused on the book or look downward or close our eyes or look outward and above or beyond the assembly.

We need to be aware of our facial expression, which communicates much to the assembly. In voice, posture, facial expression, we are prayerful, reverent, hospitable. As a criterion of our ability to deliver the spoken word, an observer, watching our posture and eye-movement and without hearing our words, should be able to tell who our audience is!

▶ *"Back in the days of the Latin Mass when the priest had his back to the congregation, he didn't have to worry about trying to be heard or understood or where he should look. But now, even though it has been many years since the presider turned around, we're still trying to deal with all the implications of that one reform."*

▶ *"At our parish the presider often memorizes the Gospel reading. Then, when it comes time for the reading he stands before us, holding the lectionary to his breast, and looking straight at us while telling the Gospel story. No matter how familiar the Scripture, it always takes on new life and meaning for me!"*

Reading Aloud

The words to be read aloud are so important that all need to be rehearsed. Everything spoken needs to be practiced with several objectives:

- for our own understanding;
- to determine how to convey meaning to others;
- to practice the pronunciation of difficult or unfamiliar words;
- to determine phrasing and emphasis for clarity;
- to establish an appropriate reading pace;
- to determine an appropriate voice level.

During this practice we might decide to mark places to pause, or to add pronunciation guides. For example, when making announcements it might be helpful to use a 3 x 5 card for pronunciation notations. For example:

> *The family of John Mishima (Mee'-shi-ma)*
> *invite you to a luncheon*
> *immediately after the committal service.*
> *The luncheon will be at the*
> *Kosciuszko (Kosh-chush'-ko) Hall,*
> *located at the intersection of*
> *LaJolla (La-Hoy'-ya) Avenue and*
> *Dubois (Du-bwa') Street.*

CONSIDER

When have you sensed that a reader was sight-reading the text? Why did you think there had been no preparation? What was your reaction?

When have you heard your name, or the name of a friend, mispronounced? What was your response?

How would you rate the quality of proclaiming Scripture in your faith community? Could it be improved? If yes, then how?

What do you foresee as a particular challenge in reading aloud as a presider? What can you do to overcome that challenge?

What special talent do you bring to this aspect of presiding?

PRAYER
PREPARATION
PRACTICE
PRAYER

When reading an announcement or sermon or Scripture, we are reading to the assembly and try to make eye contact as often as possible. We raise our head long enough to look at the assembly; that communicates to the assembly that we are speaking to them. We avoid the head-bobbing routine, where the head is raised so briefly that it resembles a reflex-action rather than a conscious movement.

Often the most challenging texts for reading aloud are the Scripture texts. The challenge extends beyond working with complex or awkward sentence structure and unfamiliar words. When we read Scripture aloud before the assembly, we participate in an activity that is basic to our tradition. According to the Gospel of Luke, Christ began his ministry by reading Scripture to those assembled in the synagogue.

▶ *"As a church organist I have played for hundreds of weddings and funerals. It's great to see the family members and close friends involved in these special services. However, I can usually tell when the reader is not an experienced lector—he or she almost always reads too fast!"*

Liturgical Language

Much of our liturgy—sometimes too much—is words. The presider and other liturgical ministers read prayers, Scripture, sermons, intercessions and announcements. The presider speaks God's message to the assembly and makes heard many of the unspoken words in the hearts and minds of those assembled.

The language we use while presiding is tremendously important, both to the liturgy and to the assembly. We use liturgical language when addressing the assembly. This is the language of the rite books, of the universal prayers of the Church. Although it is formal and stylized prayer, it is not stilted; neither is it folksy or trite. Liturgical language conveys our recognition of the value of gathering. It forms those of us who have gathered, and expresses and forms our theology. Liturgical language reminds us that we are in the presence of Holy Mystery. Through it we acknowledge that we have been called by God and cannot pray without the Holy Spirit directing and guiding us.

Liturgy, in both ritual and words, forms community. Liturgical language always addresses the assembly as a whole, not as a group of individuals. As presiders we speak as representatives of the faith community. Because the presider prays in the name of the entire community, we say "we," not "I"; we say "our" God, not "my" God.

Liturgical language is to be beautiful. Ours is a God of beauty, deserving of worship that is delightful to the eye and pleasing to the ear. Therefore the words of worship should be poetic and inspiring, eloquently expressing the community's worship of the Divine.

Liturgical language recognizes the presence and inclusion of all. The gospel message is inclusive; the love of God is radically inclusive; our liturgical actions and our liturgical language are to be inclusive.

Liturgical language, in describing or addressing God, is metaphorical and symbolic. We speak, not so much of what God is, but rather, what God is like. The Hebrew Scriptures (Old Testament) are filled with metaphors for God: God is like a rock, a fortress; God cares for us like a nursing mother; God is like light, breath, silence. No one title, form of

CONSIDER

What are the traditions in your parish concerning liturgical language? What are the strengths of these traditions? Any weaknesses? If yes, what can be done about them?

Where, in your community, is the word of God proclaimed to the hearing impaired in their own language?

What are some examples of liturgical language that is not beautiful? Not inclusive? Not appropriate to the assembly? Limiting of the God-images?

What are some examples of liturgical language that could replace those mentioned above?

While our words and art forms cannot contain or confine God, they can, like the world itself, be icons, avenues of approach, numinous presences, ways of touching without totally grasping or seizing. Flood, fire, the rock, the sea, the mountain, the cloud, the political situations and institutions of succeeding periods—in all of them Israel touched the face of God, found help for discerning a way, moved toward the reign of justice and peace. Biblical faith assures us that God covenants a people through human events and calls the covenanted people to shape human events. (Environment and Art in Catholic Worship, #2)

address or name can contain God. Therefore, in our liturgical language we are sensitive to all present and use a variety of titles: Father/Father/Parent, Alpha and Omega, Yahweh, Adonai, Life-giving Love, Wellspring of Mercy, Compassionate One, Creator/Savior/Sustainer, Weaver God, God of Tears and Laughter, Eternal Word, Lady Wisdom, Ancient Beauty, Eternal Goodness, Tree of Life and so on.

Liturgical language is to be appropriate to the assembly. In parishes that are multicultural and multilingual, the presider needs to be sensitive to the needs of all traditions. In consultation with the pastor or liturgist the presider attempts to meet those needs. If the presider is not multilingual, then someone proficient in the other language is chosen to make announcements, distribute communion, give the eulogy and so on.

Language, both in worship and in everyday life, has the power to change the world. Words can empower or restrict, encourage or dishearten, inspire or seduce, heal or wound, embrace or exclude, convey or withhold love.

▶ *"I'm so glad we no longer have the Mass in Latin. It's difficult to be prophetic in a dead language!"*

▶ *"We had gotten to the place in the rite for the Our Father. The presider then said, 'We are all God's children. Therefore, we address God as Our Creator, Our Mother, Our Father, Who art in heaven, hallowed be thy name....'"*

Scripture in Liturgy

Reading Scripture in a liturgical setting is unlike any other type of reading aloud. Scripture is not merely to be read; it is to be proclaimed. But what does that mean? As lector or presider we proclaim the word of the Lord from *The Holy Bible*, which could be subtitled "The Story of God's Love for Humanity."

To proclaim the word of God is to transform biblical stories and images in such a way that they have a significant influence in our lives today. What happened thousands of years ago does affect us now. We make alive once more the people in Scripture, that fascinating assemblage of characters that make up our historical faith-family. We bring life to the history of our faith. Our faith, our theology, our religious practices are alive, growing, developing, changing. When we know and understand where we have been, we have a clearer idea of where we are going.

When we proclaim Scripture we bring breath to poetry and offer melody to songs, not only those in the Book of Psalms, but the canticles, the prophetic oracles and other prose worthy of being called poetry. We give voice to the laws, guidelines and commands of our faith tradition and make them alive today, now, here.

People need heroes. In recounting the legends of our tradition we discover a delightfully inspiring and diverse supply of heroes and heroines. Through Scripture we retell the lasting myths of our faith. Though myths are not historically accurate, they are true in the larger sense, for they are answers to the basic human questions about the meaning of life and our relationship with the divine. Through myths we

CONSIDER

What is the place of Scripture in your life?

What are the different ways in which you read Scripture: As story? As prayer? As meditation? As poetry? As myth and legend? As inspired word?

When have you been transformed by the proclamation of the word in liturgy?

How does proclaiming the word of God differ from reading the word of God?

How do you prepare to proclaim the word of God?

What is conveyed to the assembly when the word of God is read from a loose sheet of paper? When it is read from a bound book? When it is delivered from memory?

tell the great truths of our faith; the importance and ramifications of myth would be difficult to overemphasize.

When the inspired word is proclaimed, the Spirit moves. We engage the imagination and creativity of all present, enabling them to be open to hear God's voice speaking to them. We clear the way for the assembly's encounter with the Divine. Beyond our power, beyond human endeavor, the proclaimed word quickens within those receptive to it. Beyond rational thought, the miraculous, grace-filled transformation occurs.

Proclaiming Scripture in liturgy is always alive and dynamic. All who proclaim—the lector, cantor, presider—take those words and lift them from the book, giving them sound, propelling them out to the assembly. And the Holy Spirit, moving through and in those gathered there, brings forth transformation. The word is alive and fills the worship space.

During the Responsorial Psalm the assembly assists in the proclaiming. The responsorial is not simply a musical interlude inserted between readings so that the assembly doesn't get bored listening to words. The Responsorial Psalm gives the congregation an opportunity to be part of the proclamation. The cantor gives voice to the word of the Lord, and we, the assembly, answer in proclamation.

But simply giving voice to the words of Scripture does not make it proclaiming Scripture in the liturgical sense, unless it is received. When the lector or presider practices reading the Scripture in an empty church, what is read is not "the word of the Lord" in this liturgical sense. Why? Because there is no one to receive it. Once again the role of the assembly is singled out, for the assembly is necessary to the proclamation of the word! And through our reception of the proclamation, we, the assembly, are to become the word of God.

The assembly's involvement is emphasized by a rather recent change in the simple rite following a Scripture reading. When the lectionaries were first published in the vernacular, each reading was followed by the statement "*This is* the word of the Lord" or "*This is* the gospel of the Lord" (emphasis added). Sometimes the reader, while making that statement, would hold up the lectionary for all to see.

But the United States bishops, recognizing the power of symbol, revised that rite and now the readings are followed by "The word of the Lord" or "The gospel of the Lord." The reader does not hold up the book. This change was made to emphasize the liturgical setting of the proclamation. The word of the Lord proclaimed is not confined to a book. Just as we, presider and assembly, are the Body of Christ, so, too, we, presider and assembly, are "the word of the Lord." We, not the Bible or the lectionary, are the living, active, transforming word of the Lord!

We are the Church, the people who carry the word of the Lord out into the world. We all proclaim the word of God—not just the lector, cantor, presider, preacher. And with that proclamation each of us becomes more than we really are; we are transformed into symbols of God's word! In fact, it goes beyond symbol; we become, for each other, the word of the Lord. What we do in liturgy we are for each other during the rest of the day, the remainder of the week.

Since reading Scripture during a liturgy is to be both creative and transforming, how do we prepare for such a significant event? The presider needs to develop all the skills of serving as a lector, ever-recalling that proclaiming, like presiding, is an art. Therefore we

Who or what symbolizes the word of God for you? How?

What is the most difficult aspect of proclaiming for you?

What special talents do you bring to proclaiming the word of God?

What resources are available to you for obtaining background information on Scripture?

Do you find that retyping the Scripture reading makes it easier to read with meaning?

What else would assist you in reading aloud? In proclaiming the word of God?

What assistance is available to the lectors in your faith community? What method of feedback is used to help lectors and others who read?

When the Scriptures are read in the Church, God himself speaks to his people, and it is Christ, present in his word, who proclaims the Gospel. (General Instruction on the Roman Missal, #9)

continually work at acquiring those qualities necessary for authentic presiding and reading.

Preparation of the texts for the liturgy includes praying to the Holy Spirit for wisdom and understanding, reading the texts as many days or weeks in advance as possible, letting the words and thoughts become part of us. We identify the tone and type of each reading—psalm or poetry, story, dialogue, parable or myth, commandments—as well as the main points of the readings; we summarize the texts. We look up the context and background of the reading and consult a Bible commentary for added information. We check the pronunciation of proper names and unfamiliar words. We read the texts aloud, conscious of enunciation, articulation, phrasing and pace.

It is often helpful to read to another person who is willing to be objective and offer helpful critique. If no one is available, we may want to tape the readings and then listen to the playback without the written text in front of us. This is also helpful in checking for clarity of communication.

Practice may indicate a need for marks or notes to help with phrasing or pronunciation. If we are reading from a lectionary or rite book that should not be defaced, we may be able to insert our notes on one or more Post-its. However, we may decide to retype the text (samples of retyping on pages 84-86 may suggest helps to reading aloud.)

All papers used during a liturgy should be securely ordered in a visually pleasing manner. Since a loose sheet of paper is easily misplaced or dropped, it should be inserted securely in the presider book or lectionary (peelable tape or glue is useful). Another possibility is to mount onto the inside cover of the lectionary or rite book a see-through pocket into which a copy of the reading can be inserted. Then, when the presider reads from this copy the assembly sees only the lectionary.

As final preparation the presider checks the lectionary and presider's book, ambo and sound system before the liturgy.

When it is time to proclaim we approach the ambo reverently, look out over the assembly before we begin, remain calmly aware of facial expression and body language. We pause at the end of the reading before concluding: "The word (gospel) of the Lord" and remain standing for the assembly's response: "Thanks be to God."

Looking directly into people's eyes is often interpreted as a sign of integrity and truth-telling; by looking at the assembly we indicate our desire that they accept the validity of our proclamation. We also listen while we are reading, for we are proclaiming to ourselves as well as to the assembly.

Samples of Printed Texts. These samples illustrate various ways to use the printed text to help in reading prayers or proclaiming Scripture. Practicing with different forms can help determine which kind of printing is easier to read, how different layouts can help with phrasing, how space in the printed form can be a reminder to allow space between words. Personal notes can even be included.

Personal preferences can guide our preparation of the texts of prayers, announcements, directions, sermons and other texts in a presider book.

The text that follows appears similarly to the way it is printed in the *Order of Christian Funerals* (#137, Luke 24:13-16, 28-35).

A reading from the holy gospel according to LUKE

Now that very day the first day of the week two of the disciples were going to a village seven miles from Jerusalem called Emmaus, and they were conversing about all the things that had occurred. And it happened that while they were conversing and debating, Jesus himself drew near and walked with them, but their eyes were prevented from recognizing him.

As they approached the village to which they were going, he gave the impression that he was going on farther. But they urged him, "Stay with us, for it is nearly evening and the day is almost over." So he went in to stay with them.

And it happened that, while he was with them at table, he took bread, said the blessing, broke it, and gave it to them. With that their eyes were opened and they recognized him, but he vanished from their sight. Then they said to each other, "Were not our hearts burning within us while he spoke to us on the way and opened the scriptures to us?" So they set out at once and returned to Jerusalem where they found gathered together the eleven and those with them who were saying, "The Lord has truly been raised and has appeared to Simon!" Then the two recounted what had taken place on the way and how he was made known to them in the breaking of the bread.

The gospel of the Lord.

Here is another way of laying out the text.

A reading from the holy gospel according to LUKE

Now that very day
the first day of the week
two of the disciples were going to a village
    seven miles from Jerusalem
    called Em'-ma-us,
and they were conversing about all the things that had occurred.

And it happened that while they were conversing and debating,
Jesus himself drew near
    and walked with them,
but their eyes were prevented from recognizing him.

As they approached the village to which they were going,
he gave the impression that he was going on farther.
But they urged him,
"Stay with us,
for it is nearly evening
    and the day is almost over."
So he went in to stay with them.

And it happened that,
while he was with them at table,
he took bread,
said the blessing,
broke it,
and gave it to them.

With that their eyes were opened and they recognized him,
but he vanished from their sight.

Then they said to each other,
"Were not our hearts burning within us
    while he spoke to us on the way
    and opened the scriptures to us?"

So they set out at once
and returned to Jerusalem
    where they found gathered together
    the eleven and those with them who were saying,
"The Lord has truly been raised and has appeared to Simon!"

Then the two recounted what had taken place on the way
and how he was made known to them
in the breaking of the bread.

The gospel of the Lord.

Another way of printing the text.

A reading from the holy gospel according to LUKE

NOW THAT VERY DAY
THE FIRST DAY OF THE WEEK
TWO OF THE DISCIPLES WERE GOING TO A VILLAGE
    SEVEN MILES FROM JERUSALEM
    CALLED EM'-MA-US,
AND THEY WERE CONVERSING ABOUT ALL THE THINGS
  THAT HAD OCCURRED.

AND IT HAPPENED THAT WHILE THEY WERE CONVERSING
  AND DEBATING,
JESUS HIMSELF DREW NEAR
    AND WALKED WITH THEM,
BUT THEIR EYES WERE PREVENTED FROM RECOGNIZING HIM.

AS THEY APPROACHED THE VILLAGE TO WHICH THEY WERE
  GOING,
HE GAVE THE IMPRESSION THAT HE WAS GOING ON
  FARTHER.
BUT THEY URGED HIM,

PRAYER
P**R**EPARATION
PR**A**CTICE
PRA**Y**ER

"STAY WITH US,
FOR IT IS NEARLY EVENING
AND THE DAY IS ALMOST OVER."
SO HE WENT IN TO STAY WITH THEM.

AND IT HAPPENED THAT, *(slow down)*
WHILE HE WAS WITH THEM AT TABLE,
HE TOOK BREAD,
SAID THE BLESSING,
BROKE IT,
AND GAVE IT TO THEM.

WITH THAT THEIR EYES WERE OPENED AND THEY
RECOGNIZED HIM,
BUT HE VANISHED FROM THEIR SIGHT.

THEN THEY SAID TO EACH OTHER,
"WERE NOT OUR HEARTS BURNING WITHIN US
WHILE HE SPOKE TO US ON THE WAY
AND OPENED THE SCRIPTURES TO US?"

SO THEY SET OUT AT ONCE
AND RETURNED TO JERUSALEM
WHERE THEY FOUND GATHERED TOGETHER
THE ELEVEN AND THOSE WITH THEM WHO WERE SAYING,
"THE LORD HAS TRULY BEEN RAISED AND HAS APPEARED TO
SIMON!"

THEN THE TWO RECOUNTED WHAT HAD TAKEN PLACE ON
THE WAY
AND HOW HE WAS MADE KNOWN TO THEM
IN THE BREAKING OF THE BREAD.
(pause)

The gospel of the Lord.

▶ *"Sometimes when the lector or presider begins reading Scripture I think to myself 'Oh, that familiar text.' And then the reader pauses unexpectedly or uses an unanticipated emphasis and the entire reading becomes new for me."*

▶ *"I love myths! Reading or hearing those marvelous stories—not only of Christianity or of Western cultures, but of the world—is a fascinating way to learn about different peoples or religions. How lasting are stories!"*

▶ *"I've read about people having near-death experiences and how they recognized the voices of dead friends and family members greeting them. As I thought about this I realized that when I die there will be people who will recognize* my *voice from my lectoring: Isaiah, Jeremiah, Luke, John the Evangelist."*

▶ *"My friend Mark, who is a marvelous combination of activist and*

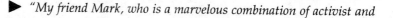

mystic, was asked to write his interpretation of the gospel. He answered, 'Look at my life! That's the only interpretation of value.' As I've thought about Mark's words I've come to realize that statement is true for all of us!"

▶ *"I attended a ministry workshop recently. At the opening prayer service the lector was a man involved with the workshop registration. As he approached the podium I noticed a phosphorescent-orange pencil stuck behind his ear! He read most earnestly—but I was mesmerized with watching that pencil bouncing up and down as the man looked from page to assembly and then back to page. I didn't hear a word of Scripture!"*

▶ *"Each year the liturgist at our parish purchases a lector's workbook for every lector. I use it for my preparation and then cut out the reading and bring it to church and tuck it into the lectionary before the liturgy. This really works for me!"*

Intercessions

In liturgy the assembly prays specifically for its own needs and the needs of others during the general intercessions or prayer of the faithful.

The form of the intercessions includes an introductory prayer by the presider; a number of intercessions read by the lector (or presider) with the response said or sung by the people; intercessions offered from the assembly if that is the local custom; a closing prayer by the presider.

If the response is something other than "Lord, hear our prayer," then the lector (or presider) leads or announces the chosen response. The response to the intercessions may also be sung; a cantor may lead it, although the assembly also responds. Singing heightens the dignity of the ritual.

Intercessions should cover these categories: the Church, the world, those in need, the local faith community. In the intercessions we recognize the whole Church and connect the local faith community with the greater family of God. The various rites books present a fine variety of intercessions for our use. Many of these are carefully honed to express eloquently our concerns and needs; they may also serve as models for additional intercessions or be adapted to fit specific situations.

If local custom includes spontaneous petitions from the assembly, then a final petition, offered by the presider, could be: "For all these intentions named, and for those that lie unspoken in our hearts, let us pray to the Lord...."

If we are called upon to write the intercessions, keep these points in mind:

- Use the intercessions in the rites books as models and adapt as appropriate;
- avoid lengthy or complicated intercessions that are difficult for the assembly to follow;
- use a repetitive wording pattern;
- do not use the same intercessions for every liturgy for they may become so familiar as to be unheard.

It should be noted that intercessions are not announcements. The follow-

---

CONSIDER

How well do you listen to the intercessions? Why?

How much do you identify with the intercessions? Why?

What kind of petitions do you think should be included in an assembly's intercessions? Why?

How would you write a set of intercessions? (Why not practice writing them?)

In the general intercessions or prayer of the faithful, the people exercise their priestly function by interceding for all mankind [sic].... As a rule the sequence of intentions is: (a) for the needs of the Church, (b) for public authorities and the salvation of the world, (c) for those oppressed by any need, (d) for the local community. In particular celebrations...the list of intentions may be more closely concerned with the special occasion. (General Instruction on the Roman Missal, #45-46)

ing examples are illustrations of how *not* to write intercessions:

> Let us pray for those who mourn the death of Maria Gonsalves, whose funeral will be celebrated here on Tuesday evening at 7 p.m., with visitation beginning at 4 p.m. and the members of the funeral committee are to contact the committee chair by Monday to plan the meal to be served in our parish dining hall following the funeral—We pray to the Lord....

> Let us pray for the return to health of Samuel Carver White who had surgery last Thursday and who is now recuperating nicely in Divine Mercy Hospital, room 607, where the visiting hours are from 2 to 8 p.m. daily—We pray to the Lord....

An example of an acceptable intercession would be:

> For the sick, the aged and the hospitalized, especially Samuel Carver White—We pray to the Lord....

The additional information can be included in the announcements at the end of the liturgy.

▶ *"Our parish liturgist chooses or writes such beautiful intercessions. And whenever I can identify with one of the groups that we are praying for, I really feel blessed. The whole community is praying for me."*

Original Prayers

We have an abundance of beautiful, touching, poetic, well-crafted prayers available for our use. These include the traditional prayers of the Church in the rites books and prayer books; the prayers of the saints, both ancient and modern; recently written creative and inspiring prayers available in books and magazines.

At times, however, either out of necessity or desire, we want to write our own prayers or use spontaneous prayer. It may be that we have no written text that seems to apply to the situation and so choose to write a unique prayer for the ritual. Or, it may be that spontaneous prayer is more appropriate.

The type of prayer and the words we use are bounded only by our imagination, for there are many different ways to pray. And we certainly are free to tap into the wellspring of metaphor and poetry and Scripture that has become part of us.

When we use original or spontaneous prayers in a liturgical setting, our prayers may quite rightfully be influenced by the readings and the sermon. We do not, however, use the prayers to give our own interpretation of the readings, nor do we use the prayers to give our own response to the sermon.

Our prayers do not preach, teach, summarize the sermon, respond to the sermon or give our own interpretation of the readings. We pray!

One prayer form that has long been part of our Catholic tradition is a useful basis for original or spontaneous prayer. This prayer form is modelled on the collect (col'-lect). This prayer gathers up or collects the petitions of the assembly and brings them to a conclusion.

A collect is characterized by four sections, which are easily remembered by the words *"You; Who; Do; Through."* *You* is our naming of

CONSIDER

How do you usually begin your prayers?

How do you usually conclude your prayers?

What are your favorite titles for God? How do you usually address God?

What past or continuing deeds of God are most significant to you?

Are you usually comfortable in using spontaneous prayer in a group? If no, why not? How can you increase your comfort level?

Will you be expected to use original or spontaneous prayers in your presiding ministry? If yes, when?

Practice writing prayers in the collect form. Try writing some practice prayers in other forms.

God, the divine address that we use, the title by which we call on God. *Who* expands on the address; we remind God—and ourselves—of past divine deeds. *Do* declares our petitions, our wants and needs. It is usually expressed in an imperative verb rather than a polite request. *Through* is one of our ritual conclusions. We say a doxology or ask the intercession of Christ and end with a verbal cue for the assembly's "Amen." This concluding cue needs to be done in a manner that communicates to the people, with voice and eye contact and gesture, that we are concluding this prayer offered in their name and they are now to indicate their approval and agreement with the prayer by an Amen.

Many prayers in the rites books are written in this form, as are the prayers at the beginning of each chapter of this book. Look, for example, at this prayer from the beginning of Chapter Five.

> *O Most Bounteous God!*
> *You have sanctified our world with beauty.*
> *Our universe dances,*
> *makes music,*
> *stirs us to tears with its splendor!*
> *Inspire us in our worship of you!*
> *Direct us in what we do—*
> *that the sound and sight*
> *and movement and touch of our liturgies*
> *may be pleasing to you*
> *and reveal yet more of you to us.*
> *We ask this in the name of Jesus the Christ,*
> *who sang and danced and prayed among us,*
> *and who is Lord for ever and ever. Amen.*

You is our naming of God: "O Most Bounteous God." *Who* expands on the address: "You have sanctified our world with beauty. Our universe dances, makes music, stirs us to tears with its splendor!" *Do* declares our petitions: "Inspire us... Direct us...." *Through* is one of our ritual conclusions: "We ask this in the name of Jesus the Christ...."

Books for Presiding

Many books may be used when planning a service or while presiding. Especially important are the lectionary, the sacramentary, the various rites books as determined by our presiding needs, the *Ordo* or the *Order of Prayers in the Liturgy of the Hours and Celebration of the Eucharist* (year) (Diocese), and finally, the presider book. Each is described in the following sections.

Lectionary. The lectionary contains the Scripture readings that have been chosen for each specific day. Before Vatican II the institutional Church placed little emphasis upon Scripture. Consequently, there were fewer Scripture readings included in the daily and Sunday liturgies and these were repeated yearly.

The Second Vatican Council recognized the importance of our becoming familiar with the Bible; as a consequence more readings were incorporated into the liturgies.

The lectionary has two sections, one for the Sundays of the year and

CONSIDER

Which of these above books are most familiar to you? Least familiar?

Where are these books available in your faith community?

How can you become more at home with these books?

What is the tradition at your parish concerning the books used by the presider? What are the advantages of that system? Are there any disadvantages? If so, how can they be minimized?

The treasures of the Bible are to be opened up more lavishly, so that a richer fare may be provided for the faithful. In this way a more representative portion of holy Scripture will be read to the people in the course of a prescribed number of years. (Constitution on the Sacred Liturgy, #51)

The power of a liturgical celebration to share faith will frequently depend upon its unity—a unity drawn from the liturgical feast or season or from the readings appointed in the lectionary as well as artistic unity flowing from the skillful and sensitive selection of options, music, and related arts. (Music in Catholic Worship, #11)

another for daily liturgies. The readings for Sundays follow a three-year rotation, known as cycles A, B and C. The readings for the daily liturgies follow a two-year rotation (Years I and II).

The assembly has the right to hear the Scriptures of the day proclaimed. Whatever service or liturgy we are planning, whatever ritual we may be doing, we should consider including one or more of the Scriptures of the day. While there certainly are exceptions, such as funerals or liturgies with children, we should at least check the lectionary for the assigned readings before choosing others.

The book used for the Scripture readings should not be used for the sermon or sermon notes or announcements. There should be no confusion about when the presider is reading Scripture and when the presider is preaching or speaking as an individual minister.

Sacramentary. In times past the sacramentary was considered the priest's book because it contains the detailed regulations concerning the Mass. But the present sacramentary is of interest to all the community, for it gives the pastoral and theological vision of the Second Vatican Council as well as the rationale for how we, as a faith community, celebrate liturgy. A familiarity with the foreword and the "General Instruction" helps establish our foundation in liturgy and theology. The sacramentary does not include the Scripture readings; these are found in the lectionary.

Ordo. The *Ordo* is the practical, little-but-official book that contains directions for those sections of the liturgy that change with the calendar and also with the geographical location. For example, we would look to the *Ordo* for the liturgical color of the feast or season, the appropriate week of the Liturgy of the Hours, the celebration of the patron of our diocese or the memorial of a locally popular saint.

Rites Books. Various books deal with the specific rites; these are mentioned by name in the chapter on rites (pages 107-127) and in the resources (pages 135-145). The introduction in each of the rites books contains a wonderful treasury of information concerning the celebration of that rite. Included in the introduction are suggestions for music, appropriate symbols and options for celebrating the rite.

Usually these options include a variety of prayers that may be used. Many of these are beautiful and poetic, adaptable to specific situations and illustrate the concern of the greater Church for the individual community and for the members of each community. They deserve our attention!

Presider Book. While we are presiding we may be using one of the published rites books. Often, however, it is helpful to put together a special presider book. This might include any or all of the following: the prayers of the rite, the music for the liturgy, specific rituals, private notations, the sermon or meditation, directions and reminders, announcements.

A presider book often is a cooperative effort between the presider and the liturgist or pastor. The benefit of such a presider book is that everything is together and in order, eliminating confusion or the need to change books. Presiders should ascertain that personal notations and reminders are included and that the type used is easily readable.

Such a presider book would not contain the readings from Scripture, for it should always be obvious to the assembly when Scripture is being read.

A presider book should be of good quality, attractive and suitable for use during a liturgy. A plain three-ring binder works well. The book could be covered in cloth and appropriately decorated.

Being Heard

All our concern about understanding and language and preparation is of little value if we can't be heard! Being heard by the assembly is a problem that is to be seriously considered and solved *before* the liturgy. Some specific steps for presiders to take include practicing speaking and reading in the worship space; practicing projecting one's voice to fill the space; testing the sound system; practicing with others present who can evaluate; arranging for one or more people to be in the assembly during the liturgy and to signal how well the presider is heard.

It is our responsibility, as presiders, to be sure we can be heard. To preface our prayer or Scripture reading by asking "Can everyone hear me?" disrupts the assembly's prayer. We step out of ritual when we do this.

It is vital that the presider be familiar with the sound system and with the microphone. This includes knowing how to turn the sound system and microphone on and off and how to work with the individual microphones. Even though a knowledgeable person is usually present during the liturgy to manage the sound system, it is prudent for the presider to be familiar with it as well.

It is also essential that the presider be at home with the particular characteristics of the microphone itself. Some need to be held close to our mouth or they will not pick up our voice; some, if we are too close to them, will distort the sound. Some have a directed pick-up of sound so that, if we turn our head away, our voice will not be amplified; others have a wide pick-up range, allowing us more freedom of head movement.

Cordless microphones that can be worn by the presider should be checked in advance. Some can be worn on a side lapel and will still amplify our voice even if we turn our head to the other side. Others must be worn directly below our mouth or we will not get an even pick-up of our voice.

While all this may seem rather complicated, these characteristics of the sound system will be readily apparent during a practice session in the worship space.

During a service we may not always be able to tell how well we are being heard in the worship space. Depending upon the size and configuration of the area, we may need to have one or more people stationed in stragetic places to communicate to us how well we are being heard. By agreeing upon signals before the liturgy begins we can get evaluation during the liturgy.

The signals should be simple, such as a "yes" nod to indicate that we are being heard at an acceptable level; a "no" head motion to indicate that the sound system is not working; a hand placed over the mouth to indicate that we are too loud; a hand cupped behind the ear to indicate

CONSIDER

How do you respond to a speaker or presider who cannot be heard? To one who does not know how to use the microphone or amplification system?

How are the acoustics and sound system in the worship spaces where you will be presiding? Do people often have difficulty being heard in those spaces? What can you do to assure that you will be heard when presiding?

What arrangements can you make to have someone communicate to you, while you are presiding, how well you are heard?

How much of our liturgies are words? Do we ever have liturgies that are too wordy? How can this be avoided?

that we need to speak louder or get closer to the microphone. Sometimes our effectiveness as a presider may come down to the practical matter of acoustics and electronics.

► *"I recently attended a week-long workshop on presiding. Considering the costs for tuition, travel, room and board, plus my contribution of time, I really resented having to contend with a cantankerous sound system. The workshop organizers knew we were coming—why weren't all the acoustical problems taken care of before we got there?"*

The Flow of the Liturgy

All the individual liturgical gestures, readings, prayers and rituals are integrated into one cohesive liturgical whole. The smooth flow of a liturgy requires the presider's attention to many details. The presider enables all the liturgical ministers and the assembly to worship together.

Trinity of Love and Delight,
Maker and Sustainer of all that is,
you know and name each atom in this universe;
you regard nothing that exists
as unworthy of your attention.
Instill in us respect for your worship.
Enliven within us
joy and awe and gratitude
that all we do
honor you,
praise you,
glorify you
throughout your creation.
We ask this through Christ, our Lord, Amen.

Before the Liturgy Begins

Our society is accustomed to pregame activities, to warmups before the main event, to the overture before the opera, to various rituals and traditions that help those present enter into the proper spirit of the occasion.

Both presider and assembly need time to prepare to celebrate liturgy. We need transition time in which to leave behind the other activities of our lives, the worries and concerns and duties that usually consume our attention; we need time to turn that concentration to the community's worship of God. This transition time immediately preceding a liturgy can greatly influence the mood, the pace, the focus, the prayerfulness of the service.

The presider should arrive early, allowing sufficient time for presiding preparation and also to be available to others who may have questions about order or cues or any other detail in the liturgy. While the presider does not do everything in the liturgy, the presider should know and understand the order of the entire liturgy.

The presider's presence and actions begin creating an environment that speaks of the sacredness of what is about to take place. The community's hospitality—or lack of it—is evidenced in the church parking lot, on the neighboring sidewalks, in the nursery and coatroom, in the hallways and gathering space and choir loft and wherever else the assembly gathers. All the sounds and activity taking place before public worship either help or hinder what follows.

One of the greatest helps in preparing for prayer is the physical

CONSIDER

What activity precedes liturgy in your parish? Does it help or hinder the liturgy?

What activity precedes liturgy in other spaces where you have liturgy? Does it help or hinder the liturgy?

What can you do, as a member of the assembly, to create an environment of activity that benefits the liturgy?

What can you do, as a presider, to create an environment of activity that enables a prayerful liturgy?

environment. An environment becomes sacred because of what we do there. Our cathedrals and churches and chapels are sacred because of the worship that takes place in these spaces; they have been made holy through the faith of the people who have worshiped there. This sacredness is usually honored within the space: banners, wall hangings, statues, paintings, wood carvings, stained glass windows and other artwork, lights, candles and flowers. When a liturgy is to take place in a church or chapel, much already exists to assist us in making the transition to public prayer.

But any space, including the nursing home dining room and the school auditorium, can become sacred through our faith in gathering there and through our actions in that space. When the liturgy is held in such a space then we use other ways to help create the worship space (see pages 43-44).

Whether in a church or temporary worship area the sacredness of the space is also determined by our reverence within that space. How we deport ourselves, how we move, how and when we tend to our duties—all these things convey to others (and reinforce for ourselves) our regard for the space. Thus, just as the physical environment may help or hinder our public prayer, so too does our activity before the service.

This activity is apparent in the typical Sunday liturgy. Each faith community has an established pattern for arrival. The specific order and times may vary, but generally there are those who arrive early: custodians, ushers, music people, liturgical ministers, some members of the assembly. The majority of the assembly generally arrive later.

The early people often have special functions before that liturgy and how those duties are performed can greatly affect the liturgy. Once the faith community begins to assemble, then the activity in the space becomes part of the environment, either helping or hindering the assembly in making the transition to public worship.

This time before is necessarily one of movement. People are gathering, greeting friends, finding favorite seats, getting worship aids or hymnals, tending to young children. It is not a time of silence. If we have community then people greet one another and express their care for each other.

Liturgical ministers can certainly engage in normal movement. Keep in mind, however, that galloping across the front aisle, running nervously from sacristy to sanctuary to choir area, juggling an armload of items from gathering space to altar area, vigorously chomping on chewing gum while passing out worship aids, whipping around microphone cords, yelling across the sanctuary space, tuning instruments and hurriedly rearranging altar furniture are distracting.

The ministers of the liturgy need to remember that while they are concerned about their various duties, the assembly is also trying to prepare for its duty: worship. All the preparatory tasks should be done in a manner that recognizes the sacredness of what is to come. For example, lighting altar candles with a pocket lighter certainly is efficient; if done early, it is acceptable. However, if the candles are lit just before the liturgy begins then the "flick of the Bic" detracts from the sacredness of the event. At this time, the candle lighting should be considered part of the ritual and be done with a taper.

It may be necessary to test the microphone or sound system; any questions concerning the sound system should be resolved before the liturgy begins. However, this, too, should be done early, since a booming "Testing, one, two, three, testing..." is definitely intrusive.

If the liturgy is not in the parish's worship space, we may have to transport needed items in a container. When we arrive at the place of worship, however, we avoid plunking the bag or carton on the temporary altar for unloading. Unpacking our items elsewhere and then reverently carrying them to the altar conveys to those present that this space, along with the temporary altar and the ritual items, are all sacred.

Any and all duties done immediately preceding the liturgy should be done reverently and ritually. Items carried to the altar are carried respectfully and with both hands. The altar is reverenced when we pass in front of it. An environment of hospitality is maintained.

Ideally there is a natural flow from the time before the liturgy to the time of the liturgy. Announcements, music rehearsal, distribution of worship aids and other such activities should take place early enough so that time remains for quiet preparation before the liturgy.

Again, what transpires in the worship space and environs immediately before the liturgy can have a profound effect upon that liturgy.

▶ *"Recently I visited a nearby Methodist church. I parked about a block away from the building and by the time I entered the church I had been greeted by at least a dozen people—people I did not know but who recognized me as a stranger to the faith community. Everyone I met was warm, friendly, inviting. We Catholics certainly could use some of that hospitality!"*

Beginning the Liturgy

We anticipate something special as we begin our liturgy.

As a general rule, liturgies should begin at the time scheduled. Late starts often indicate lack of consideration for the assembly, and the liturgy is the assembly's prayer.

There are always exceptions. The arrival of the assembly may be delayed due to weather conditions or traffic tie-ups. If the entryway or gathering space is filled with people arriving for liturgy, then perhaps we should consider delaying the start of the liturgy. But we who serve the assembly should always be prepared to begin on time.

Since a well-prayed liturgy requires the combined efforts of everyone present, the decision to start is not a power play or an exercise in authority. The decision to begin the liturgy should be a cooperative one and agreed upon in advance.

The person to give the actual signal that communicates "We now begin" is usually determined by practicality: Who is in the best location to ascertain that the environment, the presider and those in the entrance procession, the musicians, the lectors and the faith community are ready? This is the person to give the signal to begin the liturgy.

In some occasions it is not obvious just when the liturgy starts. For instance, in a nursing home or funeral chapel there may not be an entrance procession and the presider may already be seated in the worship space, while background music serves to gather the assembly. If the presider then makes announcements and immediately begins the

CONSIDER

How do you feel about liturgies, meetings, classes, performances and events that consistently begin late?

What is the tradition in your parish for beginning on time?

Who is in the best location to signal the beginning of a liturgy in your parish worship space? In the chapel? In the hospice or nursing home? In other places where you participate in public worship?

liturgy, this interrupts what has already begun. It would be preferable to make the announcements and then have the music continue for a brief time to allow the mental regathering for communal prayer; after that quiet time, the presider begins the liturgy.

▶ *"I am so pleased that we have a video of our daughter's wedding—the music was beautiful, the readings were done well, and there were so many details that seemed just right! But also recorded on that tape are the eight (I counted) times during the liturgy that the presider blatantly looked at his watch! It was annoying during the wedding and gets even more annoying with each viewing!"*

Pace and Time

We, as presiders, set the pace for the liturgy through the speed at which we read, pray, speak and move. We set the pace through the rapidity with which we proceed from one element of the liturgy to the next. This rhythm of action is contagious; the other ministers and the assembly will usually continue in the same mode.

How does a presider develop a feel for what is a comfortable and reverent pace? One of the easiest ways is through careful observation of experienced presiders who are able to enter into prayerful public worship. Such observation will usually yield several conclusions: The entrance procession that looks reverent probably moves at a pace slower than first realized; the reading, praying and speaking rates are also slower than are first apparent; there is more silence during the liturgy than most people later recall.

Just as the inexperienced lector usually reads too fast, the inexperienced presider usually moves, reads and prays too fast. This rapid pace may be due to nervousness or to a desire to get through it quickly. If the presider is anxious to get through the liturgy, however, then most likely the presider is not *in* the liturgy!

This brings us back to the consideration of presence (see page 19). Being present to the liturgy and to presiding means not rushing through the liturgy, presiding at a reverent pace out of respect for the liturgy itself, presiding at an appropriate pace out of consideration for the assembly, realizing that silence is needed after a reading or the sermon, recognizing that pauses are necessary during or following ritual actions. Above all we need to recognize that the presider is the servant of the liturgy and of the assembly.

The presider's guideline is always what best assists the assembly's prayer.

A presider must be aware of both *chronos* time and *kairos* time (see "Time," pages 48-49). As much as we would like to forget about time whenever the assembly is at prayer, that is rarely feasible. There are occasions when the reality of *chronos* time puts strict limitations upon our experience of *kairos* time in liturgy. For example, Evening Prayer is scheduled to be completed in time for those attending to pick up the children from the parish religion classes. Or the morning Word-Communion liturgy is to be completed in time for people to catch the bus to work. Or the people attending the funeral service are to be out of the worship space before the guests arrive for the wedding scheduled later.

CONSIDER

How do you react when a presider is in a hurry? How do you react when a presider is too slow?

Who are some presiders you know who have a comfortable pace? How would you describe a "comfortable pace"?

How can you, as a presider, determine a comfortable pace for the liturgy?

What are some particulars that keep you in *chronos* time during a liturgy? What factors help you enter into *kairos* time during a liturgy?

How do you, as a member of the assembly, respond emotionally to a presider in a hurry?

Are you a habitual watch-checker? What do you do when you are presiding?

What presiding task do you find most difficult to do at a reverent pace?

Sometimes we do have to be concerned about time. Unfortunately, one common way of handling such a situation is with a sense of hurry: The presider rushes the liturgy. Hurrying from place to place throughout the liturgy may possibly cut twenty seconds from the length of the service, but those seconds come at a tremendous cost. Each lope or run across the sanctuary counteracts a prayerful environment. Rushing the start of the next prayer or reading conveys a sense of hurry. These actions prevent the assembly's immersion into *kairos* time.

So how do we respond when we must be concerned about the reality of time? How do we deal with liturgies that have time constraints? The answer is simple: We solve that problem *before* the liturgy. While planning the service we carefully consider the duration of each element in the liturgy, deciding what, if anything, to shorten or eliminate. We also notify the other ministers of the time constraint. Before the liturgy begins, we make certain that it will be an acceptable length.

This may entail making a number of adjustments such as shortening the sermon or the number of intercessions. During the liturgy, however, these adaptations are carried out without references to the time factor. We avoid mentioning to the assembly our time constraint, because every reference to time takes us out of ritual and disrupts the assembly's prayer.

Depending upon the situation, it may be hospitable to announce before the liturgy begins that it will be completed within the time limit. In our role as minister of hospitality, we as presiders assume the task of "watching the time" by having planned a liturgy of an appropriate length; we then are faithful to our commitment, thus freeing the assembly to enter into *kairos* time.

To nurture the assembly's experience of *kairos* time, we let the echo of the assembly's singing fade before beginning the next prayer; the lector lets the last chord of the psalm accompaniment be transformed into silence before beginning to read; we let the lector return to his or her seat before continuing with the ritual.

We allow time for the natural flow of one ritual action into another. We allow time for silence and for moments of grace. If we rush these transition times, each premature ending of silence or the absence of silence communicates *hurry* and keeps everyone in *chronos* time.

One other point to remember, whether we are in a time constraint or not, is to avoid looking at our watch. Some people, out of habit, check the time frequently. But seeing the presider look at a watch during the liturgy can disrupt the assembly's prayer and should be avoided. If necessary, remove your watch when presiding to avoid consulting it during the liturgy.

Choreography

Choreography? Isn't that about dancing? What does that have to do with presiding? Even when there is no liturgical dancer the presider has to be concerned about choreographing the liturgy. We need to attend to the details of how we and all others involved in the liturgy move throughout the course of that liturgy. Choreography is the name given to that task.

Choreography of the liturgy would involve how the worship space is prepared, how the assembly and the liturgical ministers enter into the

CONSIDER

As you observe the flow of liturgy what details have you become aware of for the first time? What details are difficult for you to envision?

How can you become more aware of the choreographic details of liturgy? Which seem most important? Why? Which seem less important? Why?

What are you most self-conscious doing as a presider? Why?

How well do you think on your feet? What do you worry about most with respect to presiding? Why?

worship space, how those involved move from point A to point B to point C during the liturgy, how the various ritual items are brought into the space, where they are placed, how they are used, how they are removed or where they remain and how the assembly and the liturgical ministers leave the worship space.

Attending to these details informs people of what they are to do and prevents awkward incidents of ministers bumping into one another or misplacing items needed for the ritual. Enumerating these details prevents misunderstandings about ministering duties and assists the smooth flow of the liturgy.

For a familiar liturgy held in the community's usual worship space, much of the choreography has been determined by tradition; the presider only has to be sure that everyone knows what those details are.

When presiding in a different space, however, such as a mortuary or senior center or school gymnasium, all these details demand our attention. The choreography would begin with the preparation of the worship space and continue through each part of the liturgy.

The easiest way to choreograph a liturgy is to walk through the service. While this may be done anywhere, it is preferable to do it in the actual space, practicing with the books and the ritual items to be used in the liturgy. That makes it easier to note details such as when to pick up the presider's book, when to put it down, when to get the incense, when to hand the book to the assistant to hold, when to stand for a prayer, when to signal for the assembly to stand and so on.

Each item or ritual in the liturgy usually involves several decisions. For instance, decisions to be made concerning the entrance procession include who is in the procession, who decides when to begin the music for the procession, what the signal to begin the procession is to be and who gives it, who leads, what the pace will be, what items are carried in the procession and who carries them, how the altar is reverenced, what is the course of movement for each of the ministers after the altar is reverenced, who begins the next part of the liturgy and when.

Again, when the liturgy is familiar and is held in the usual worship space, much of this has already been decided and the presider's main responsibility is to ascertain that everyone understands the plan.

As an example of choreographic details, consider Evening Prayer. Often this liturgy begins with subdued lighting; then, after the greeting, the lighting is gradually intensified. This involves a number of decisions: who attends to the worship space lighting before the liturgy; who attends to the overhead lighting during the liturgy; how much the overhead lighting is to be increased; who lights the extra candles; locating a taper for the lighting; where the taper is lit; the order of the candle-lighting; how long the lighting takes; whether music accompanies the candle-lighting; who decides when to end the music.

We need to consider such details if the assembly's prayer is to go smoothly.

One last word on choreography: All who move in the course of the liturgy are to do so reverently, slowly and gracefully. Many errors and much confusion can be concealed by moving slowly and reverently.

▶ *"I was the cantor for the Christmas evening liturgy. When the visiting presider turned to greet the people I groaned inwardly. This was immediately off to a bad start, for there would obviously be continuing warfare between his stole and the cord of the lapel mike. Then the presider, noticing a shortage of wine for the assembly, sent an acolyte back to the sacristy for more wine, not knowing that it had been consumed at the preceding liturgies. Deciding to solemnize the liturgy with incense, he sent the remaining acolyte for charcoal, which proved difficult to light. At the presentation of gifts, with both servers gone, the presider marched off the altar, leaving the assembly seated before an unpeopled sanctuary. In the sacristy he confronted his unsuccessful couriers: 'What's going on back here?' he demanded, his mike booming the confrontation to the startled assembly!"*

Assistants (Servers)

The liturgical reforms following the Second Vatican Council still continue. Faith communities celebrate a greater variety of liturgies, including Morning Prayer and Evening Prayer. Lay ministries have increased and now include lay presiding and lay preaching. The assembly is beginning to recognize its full and proper role in liturgy.

All these changes influence the decisions involving liturgy and presiding. As an example, there is the matter of whether to include assistants (servers) in our liturgy planning. An assistant adds solemnity to the celebration, enables the presider to be more effective and more hospitable, enhances the smooth flow of the liturgy, provides more flexibility in the liturgy, makes it easier for the presider to use the *orans* posture. An assistant also eliminates the appearance that the presider is presenting a one-person show.

The decision concerning assistants should be based on the local tradition, the liturgy itself, the rituals involved and the other particulars of the situation. What is not a factor in the decision is that the presider is a member of the laity rather than an ordained cleric.

▶ *"Kevin doesn't want to 'bother' with an assistant—yet he doesn't plan well enough to preside gracefully alone. Recently, at the closing prayer, Kevin was seated with the presider's book open on his lap. He didn't want to close it because he has trouble finding the right place—he doesn't 'bother' using markers either. But the closing prayer was in another book, which lay open on the next chair. So Kevin sat there, with one book open on his lap, leaning over to read the prayer in the other book."*

One Thing at a Time

Many of us lead fragmented and harried lives. Too busy with our multiple commitments, we carry out one task while planning the next. We overfill our days by intermeshing several tasks simultaneously; we feel inefficient if we are not doing several things at one time.

All these characteristics describe *chronos* time, however, and liturgy is to be celebrated in *kairos* time. One way of entering into prayerful presiding is by doing one thing at a time. Only if we do one thing at a time can we be present to that action or those words and express our intentions and purposes. Also, doing more than one thing at a time gives conflicting signals to the assembly.

Like most guidelines, there are exceptions: We do sing while we process (we have music for the journey); we do say the words that accompany ritual actions, such as making the sign of the cross while saying a blessing.

Whatever the presider does communicates to the assembly. When we pray, our posture, voice, eyes and hands should communicate prayer. The same unity of body and word should mark all our actions as presiders. We do not, therefore, adjust attire while processing, say the words of greeting while repositioning the microphone, "say" a prayer while picking up the presider book or paging through the hymnal or looking for the announcement list.

We do not begin speaking before we arrive at the designated place. We do not look at the person responsible for the next liturgical task before the appropriate time (being people of faith means not only having faith in God but also having faith in others).

Such distracting actions communicate to the congregation the presider's lack of presence to the liturgy and to the role of presider.

▶ *"We have one presider who is always anticipating—she never seems fully present to the current activity. For instance, if the liturgy is to begin at the foot of the altar, instead of processing in, bowing and then turning to the assembly, she walks halfway up the aisle, then turns and walks backward the remaining distance. Or, nearing the end of one prayer she starts paging through the book for the next. And when we sing a hymn she begins the next prayer while the organist is still holding the final chord. It's all very annoying!"*

What particular actions of a presider make you feel that he or she is not present to the liturgy?

How can you prepare and practice so as to be present when you are presiding?

Could you try doing only one thing at a time in your daily life? How much effort would that take? What might result from adopting this habit?

Both Hands

A corollary to "Do only one thing at a time" is "Use both hands." In our daily lives we juggle dishes and tools, books and files, kids and pets, schedules and timecards and reports. Such diversifying of ourselves may be the only way our life works.

But liturgical presiding calls for a different approach. We are to concentrate our attention on what we are doing; we are to concentrate our attention on what is happening in the liturgy. Using both hands for our liturgical task helps us focus on one thing—that task. Using both hands adds solemnity and reverence to that task, communicating its importance to the assembly. For example, when carrying or holding a book, we use both hands. When assuming the *orans* posture or greeting the assembly, we use both hands.

In our preparatory walk-through of the liturgy, we may discover instances when we are not able to use both hands to do a task. Then, in order to perform the ritual tasks in a fitting and graceful manner we may need an assistant or a different arrangement of the liturgical environment. Or we may need to memorize certain words of the liturgy.

For example, at the opening greeting of the liturgy the common gesture for the presider is to extend both hands, open and outward toward the assembly. It does not "work" if the presider has to hold the book to read the words, and a half-gesture (using one hand) is not

CONSIDER

Do you feel that your life is fragmented or too busy? Does "juggling" frequently occur in your life? How do you respond to that?

Does it seem awkward to use both hands to carry a book or to perform other ritual actions? Why?

How do you feel about memorizing some of the words of a rite? What are the advantages of doing that? Are there any disadvantages?

acceptable. So, the presider may choose to have an assistant hold the book or arrange for a book stand or memorize the words of the greeting.

Many liturgies close with a blessing. If the presider has to hold the book in one hand and make the Sign of the Cross with the other the ritual looks awkward. Again, the presider may choose to have an assistant or a book stand or memorize the words of the blessing.

In the Word-Communion service the presider presents the bread to the assembly with the words: "This is the Lamb of God who takes away the sins of the world. Happy are those who are called to his supper." The ritual calls for the presentation of the individual bread along with the vessel containing the rest of the consecrated bread. Holding up a piece of bread in one hand while balancing the presider book in the other diminishes the solemnity of the moment. The assembly might justifiably wonder if the presider really knows or believes the proclamation about the bread. While the presider may choose to have an assistant hold the book or arrange for a book stand, it would certainly be preferable to memorize the words of the ritual in order to proclaim them to the assembly with conviction.

Staying in the Ritual

One of the most common ways in which the presider transgresses the guidelines of good presiding is by not staying in the ritual. Once the liturgy begins, we stay in the ritual, which means that all our actions and words support the assembly's prayer. When we step out of ritual we interrupt that prayer.

How does the presider interrupt the assembly's prayer by stepping out of the ritual? This can be done by undesirable movement and action: moving in a less than reverent manner, such as taking the altar steps two at a time; glaring at an erring liturgical minister or grimacing at a mistake; handling the ritual items in an inappropriate way, such as slamming shut the presider's book; looking heavenward when the cantor sings a wrong note.

While all these actions disrupt ritual, the most common way of stepping out of ritual is through speech, especially through the momentary abandonment of liturgical language. The presider's words have great potential for taking everyone out of *kairos* time and interrupting worship. Often these "out of ritual" occurrences are inappropriate attempts at humor and lack both hospitality and Christian sensitivity.

Here are some examples:

The lector has completed the reading and returns to the assembly. The presider, upon reaching the ambo, discovers that the lector has turned several extra pages. When the correct reading has been located, the presider, glancing at the lector, announces to the assembly, "Some people can't turn just one page."

There is a confusion about cues and the cantor is late beginning the responsorial psalm. As the cantor approaches the microphone, the presider comments, "Better late than never!"

The assembly, unfamiliar with the Morning Prayer liturgy, is slow to stand at a specific point in the liturgy. The presider says, "Time to wake up, people!"

CONSIDER

When have you observed a presider stepping out of the ritual? What was the effect upon the assembly's prayer? What was your response?

What, in your opinion, is the reason that a presider steps out of ritual?

Are there valid reasons for interrupting the liturgy? What are some situations that call for the presider to step out of ritual? Why?

Are there ways that a presider could handle these situations and remain in ritual? How would you handle these situations if you were presiding?

Such stepping out of ritual demeans the assembly's prayer and focuses the assembly's attention upon the presider. Once the liturgy has begun, then the words and actions of the presider should all be in harmony with the liturgy.

There are instances—thankfully rare—when the presider does need to step out of ritual: the assistant has a profuse nosebleed; the altar cloth is touching the candle flame; six emergency vehicle sirens are blaring near the building.

However, even these interruptions in our presiding, if handled with consideration for both the liturgy and the assembly, can have minimal adverse impact upon the assembly's prayer.

Following the interruption, we gently draw the people's attention back to the reasons we gathered for worship. With voice tone, gestures and words we remind the assembly of our need for prayer; then we resume the liturgy.

▶ *"The workshop on biblical storytelling was nearing conclusion when word was brought in of the assassination of a well-known person of peace. The presider immediately responded with her own very moving spontaneous prayer, followed by communal silence. Then she graciously gave the microphone to others to address the tragedy. Many did, some tearfully. Eventually, the presider called us back to our reasons for gathering, placing this horrible experience in the context of the day and our deep need for the life stories of those who have gone before us, of those who live in our time. The news bulletin became another reminder of humanity's need for rituals and heroes and stories."*

CONSIDER

What cues are usually used at your parish?

What kind of cues distract the assembly from its prayer?

What is your response, as a member of the assembly, to cues and directions that you believe are unnecessary?

Have you ever felt demeaned by the presider's cues? If yes, why? How can you, as presider, avoid making the same mistake?

How do you feel when, as a member of the assembly, you don't know what is expected? How could the presider have prevented such confusion?

Cues

The main minister of the liturgy is the assembly. The assembly as a whole is involved in the liturgy, assisted by individuals as readers, cantors, liturgical dancers, instrumentalists, choir members, sacristans, assistants, greeters, ushers, presiders and others. The liturgy is never a one-person event.

Thus, as minister of hospitality, the presider often needs to give cues or signals to the assembly and to the other ministers for when to begin and end their specific involvement, when to stand and sit, when to be still and when to tend to duties. The responsibility for the coordination of the service is part of the presider role. The goal is to give these cues gracefully and graciously, in a manner that does not detract from the assembly's prayer.

In giving cues we avoid two extremes. The first is directing all the ministers and the assembly in absolutely everything they are to do; the opposite extreme is not communicating anything to anyone. To be hospitable, the presider needs to find an empowering balance in giving cues.

Giving directions for everything is distracting and can also seem demeaning. We rightly assume that the assembly knows something about its own liturgy. At the other extreme, if no cues are given or if they are too subtle, then people are distracted from their praying by wondering what they are supposed to be doing. This results in the community's prayer being diminished by confusion and uncertainty.

What kind of cues to the ministers distract the assembly from its prayer?

What are other nonverbal cues that work?

Cues to the Assembly. The degree of cue-giving to the assembly is determined by the particulars of each liturgy. If the service is a familiar one and the gathered assembly is from the local faith community, then cue-giving may be kept to a minimum. In such an instance, a visitor or new member can easily follow what the rest of the assembly does; they are already united in ritual.

If the liturgy itself is not familiar to all in the assembly—for example, an Evening Prayer incorporated into a parish mission—then more cues may be needed. Likewise, when the assembly is not one that gathers regularly—often the case for a funeral or funeral vigil—then in the name of hospitality the presider would give more cues, taking care to give them in a way that does not interrupt the ritual.

Directions and cues are to be given graciously. The presider does not need exaggerated cheerleading hand signals to communicate to the assembly. A simple nod of the head usually is sufficient to convey to the congregation it is time to be seated. To indicate to the congregation that it is time to stand the presider can extend both hands, palms upward, and then raise them.

Cues may also be given verbally. We take care to choose the words wisely, to be considerate of the assembly and to use a pleasant, not bossy, tone of voice. The invitation: "Will the Church please rise" not only gives a direction in a hospitable manner but also affirms the assembly as the Church.

Cues to Other Ministers. It is easy for presiders to slip into the emcee syndrome, directing the attention of the assembly to the next focal point of the liturgy. It seems so simple to decide that the presider should point to or look at the reader or cantor when it is time for the reading or the psalm. But this type of cue has two significant drawbacks: It unnecessarily emphasizes the presider's role, and it may result in the congregation's attention being directed prematurely to the other individual.

When the presider looks out into the assembly and then nods to the lector, the people's attention will normally follow the presider's focus. This puts the lector immediately in the spotlight. It is preferable to agree on a different cue so that the lector can make a gradual transition, when he or she is ready, into the assembly's spotlight. This allows for those valuable seconds of privacy to loosen collar, adjust belt, pat hair, put away the extra copy of the reading and do all those little things that relieve nervousness or help one prepare for the task.

If the presider has decided that the cue for the cantor is: "When I look at you, begin" the cantor or the other musicians may not be immediately ready to hit that first note. Thus their last minute preparation-flurry is spotlighted for the entire assembly.

How can we give better and more effective cues? Some general guidelines may help: The cue must be agreed upon before the liturgy; the cue does not take anyone out of ritual; the cue does not prematurely direct the assembly's attention to the other minister before that person is ready.

Some examples of nonverbal cues that work include the following: When the cantor and assembly finish singing the psalm, then the lector moves to the ambo; when the presider stands, then the musicians begin the introduction; when the presider sits down, then...; when the assistant removes the book, then...; when the presider and the assistant arrive at the designated point, then...; when the presider closes the presider book, then....

Using such actions as cues does not emphasize to the assembly the presider's role. And of course the flow of the liturgy is smoother when all these cues are agreed upon before the liturgy begins.

Sometimes a verbal cue can be given to both the assembly and the ministers. These are usually more appropriate at liturgies where the assembly is not primarily that of the established faith community. For example, "We shall now be seated for the Scripture reading" gives cues to the congregation and to the reader. "You are invited to join in the singing of the psalm" gives cues to the assembly and the musicians. "As we move into the worship space we will pass the baptismal font. Just as we need refreshment on life's journey let us now refresh ourselves in the waters of baptism. Through that water we were baptized into God's holy people!" That cue is a direction, an invitation and an affirmation of the assembly.

As we become more experienced in presiding, we become sensitive to where the focus of the assembly is directed and to when cues and directions are needed. We want the liturgy to flow smoothly without distracting words or unnecessary directions.

▶ *"At a recent anointing liturgy we sang the Litany of the Saints. The cantor sang the first part of each intercession and we answered with the traditional response. The cantor gave the hand signal for the first few responses—that was fine. But we called upon lots and lots of saints— and the cantor signaled with his hand for every single 'Pray for us'! I wanted to yell at him—'We know what we're supposed to do—we're not stupid!' Meanwhile, the cantor's arm was going up and down like a malfunctioning parking lot gate!"*

When Things Go Wrong

CONSIDER

When have you observed presiders handling problems well? Why do you consider those responses good?

When have you observed presiders handling problems poorly? Why do you consider those responses poor?

What do you most fear happening when you are presiding? Why? What's the worst possible outcome of that situation?

What do you think God's response to all these situations might be? Why?

No matter how well we pray, prepare and practice, things do, on occasion, go wrong. Something is dropped, a page is missing from the presider's book, the lighted charcoal for the incense burns out, a music stand collapses, someone misses a cue, the sound system lets forth anguished shrieks, or other interesting and unpredictable events occur. How do we, as presiders, respond?

We always begin with the assumption that the assembly is at prayer. It is possible that what disturbs the presider receives only marginal notice from the praying assembly. Often people are distracted not by the error or crisis itself but by the mishandling of it.

That observation presents us with our guide: When things go wrong we reverently and prayerfully do what is least disruptive to the assembly's prayer. This means we put aside trying to make ourselves look innocent or trying to let the assembly know who is at fault. We avoid commenting on the problem unless absolutely necessary. We do not step out of ritual. We maintain an atmosphere of love.

Reverently and prayerfully responding to the interruption can quite effectively cover a multitude of problems. Many mishaps, omissions, accidents and moments of confusion can be covered gracefully and with a minimum of disruption to the assembly's prayer if those involved, especially the presider, refrain from overreacting and finger-pointing.

On the other hand, some disruptions should be noted. If there's a hippopotamus (either literal or figurative) in the sanctuary then the presider should recognize its presence—for surely the assembly is already aware of it. Thankfully such occurrences are rare. But when they do occur, humor is often a good response to them. Our God is a God of surprises, of humor, of forgiveness, of laughter, of love. We should not be more solemn than our God!

Remember, the best time for dealing with mistakes is before the liturgy.

Presiding for the Rites

O ur Catholic tradition abounds in compelling and poetic prayers, rituals rich in symbols, spirituality that permeates all of life. These have long been ours; we have only to claim them. The variety of rites and rituals available to us reflects the concern of the institutional Church for the individual faith community and for us, the people of God, who are the Church.

Divine Savior and friend,
our teacher,
our mentor,
our light and our hope—
you promised to be with us
whenever we gather to pray.
Help us to see you
in all that is true,
in all that is loving,
in all that is beautiful,
in all that is real,
in all that is life.
Help us to see you in everyone!
Embrace us in your benediction,
for you live and reign
in the company of our Maker
and the Holy Flame of Love,
one God, for ever and ever. Amen

CONSIDER

The Second Vatican Council placed much emphasis upon the importance and value of the Liturgy of the Hours. What place does this liturgy have in your faith community? Why?

What place does the Liturgy of the Hours have in your own faith life? Why?

What can you do to make the Liturgy of the Hours a more significant element within your faith community?

Why do you think that the Liturgy of the Hours has not become more popular? What appeals to you about the Liturgy of the Hours? Is there anything you dislike about it?

The Liturgy of the Hours

The Liturgy of the Hours, or the Divine Office, has been preserved for centuries in monasteries and convents. The traditional form begins with services called Matins and Lauds, which are prayed after midnight; Prime is said at the first hour of daylight; the so-called "little hours" of Terce, Sext and None are said during the day; Vespers is the evening service; Compline marks the end of the day. With the Liturgy of the Hours the Church literally prays the clock around.

The Liturgy of the Hours is ritual prayer that focuses on praising God; it glories in creation and in God, our Creator. The Liturgy of the Hours, more than any other non-eucharistic devotion, unites us with the entire Church and sanctifies the gift of time.

This liturgy, with its roots in Judaism and its monastic nurturing, is considered by the Church to be second only to the Eucharist in our worship of God. Yet, before the Council, it was little known to ordinary laypeople and rarely prayed communally outside the monastic environs.

One of the goals of the Second Vatican Council was to revise and renew the Liturgy of the Hours to make it adaptable for broader use, especially in parishes. Although the revision of the Liturgy of the Hours

P**R**AYER
P**R**EPARATION
PR**A**CTICE
PRA**Y**ER

was accomplished in 1970, it has had only modest increase in popularity and remains one of the undervalued and unappreciated spiritual treasures of Catholicism. It has yet to be widely claimed by the People of God.

Because it does not require an ordained presider, this service is often used in place of weekday Mass, or for special group celebrations when a priest is not available for Mass. But the thrust to revitalize the Liturgy of the Hours preceded the current shortage of priests. No law, either of God or of the Church, dictates that every time Catholics gather for worship the liturgy must be that of Eucharist, even though our practice in years past has been to celebrate most occasions with a eucharistic liturgy.

The recent revisions of the Liturgy of the Hours place greater emphasis on Morning and Evening Prayer than on the other "hours." Morning and evening have long been traditional times of prayer. Our ancestors in faith rejoiced each morning that God had once again chosen to have the sun journey across the face of the flat earth. God had blessed them with the gift of one more day. And in the evening, they gave thanks for that never-to-return day and prayed for protection throughout the darkness of the night.

Although we now realize the astronomical errors of their thinking, we remain grateful to God for the gift of the day just begun; we offer prayers for protection throughout the coming night. We express, in the Liturgy of the Hours, our inconceivable surprise of living!

One of the advantages of the Liturgy of the Hours is its flexibility. It is a form of worship that can be adapted for a variety of occasions: daily worship, additional liturgies during Lent and Advent, Morning Prayer on the "high holy days" of Triduum (Holy Thursday, Good Friday, Holy Saturday) when the main liturgy is in the evening, Evening Prayer as a fitting conclusion to Triduum on Easter Sunday. Morning or Evening Prayer may be used for funeral services (see *Order of Christian Funerals*). Morning and Evening Prayer can bracket and encompass a community activity such as a workshop, lecture, day of recollection. A healing service, a school ritual, a memorial service and other creative rituals can be incorporated into Morning or Evening Prayer. Morning or Evening Prayer may be used for a Sunday observance in the absence of a priest (see *Sunday Celebrations in the Absence of a Priest*).

The basic outline for Morning and Evening Prayer is as follows:

- Introductory Verse
- Hymn
- Psalmody
- Reading
- Responsory
- Canticle
- Intercessions
- The Lord's Prayer
- Concluding Prayer
- Dismissal

Since the Liturgy of the Hours is based upon the psalms—the songs of the bible—music forms an integral part of the service. The Liturgy of the Hours has been sung in convents and monasteries for centuries; its beauty and consolation and peace belong in each faith community today.

The number of psalms may vary. Each psalm is followed by a psalm-

---

How do you feel about presiding for Morning or Evening Prayer? Why?

If the faithful come together and unite their hearts and voices in the Liturgy of the Hours, they manifest the Church celebrating the mystery of Christ. (Liturgy of the Hours, #22)

In the Liturgy of the Hours, the Church for the most part prays with those beautiful songs composed under the inspiration of the Spirit of God by the sacred authors of the Old Testament. From the beginning they have had the power to raise men's [sic] minds to God, to evoke in them holy and wholesome thoughts, to help them to give thanks in time of favor, and to bring consolation and constancy in adversity. (Liturgy of the Hours, #100)

The Holy Spirit, who inspired the psalmists, is always present with his grace to those believing Christians who with good intention sing and recite these songs.... The psalms are not readings nor were they specifically composed as prayers, but as poems of praise.... Whilst certainly offering a text to our mind, the psalm is more concerned with moving the spirit of those singing and listening, and indeed of those accompanying it with music. (Liturgy of the Hours, #102-103)

What the Second Vatican Council said with regard to singing in the Liturgy applies to every liturgical action but especially to the Liturgy of the Hours.... Singing in the Liturgy of the Hours is not to be regarded as something merely ornamental or extrinsic to prayer. It springs from the depths of the person praying and praising God, and fully and perfectly reveals the communal character of Christian worship. (Liturgy of the Hours, #69, 270)

prayer. The psalm may be sung with cantor and assembly in responsorial mode or the psalm may be sung or recited by the assembly in an alternating manner, such as by those seated on the right and left sides of the worship space.

Morning or Evening Prayer usually includes one Scripture reading. This may be taken from the lectionary for the day or the proper reading from the Liturgy of the Hours may be used. A reading appropriate for the occasion could also be chosen.

Numerous editions of the Liturgy of the Hours are available, some including only Morning and Evening Prayer. These can be used with groups, with the prayers or psalms read by individuals or sections of the assembly.

The complete Liturgy of the Hours for the entire liturgical year is also available as a set; this is mainly directed to communities that celebrate the full Liturgy of the Hours daily.

In addition, many of the newer hymnals have sections devoted to Morning and Evening Prayer that can easily be adapted for use in the parish or by small groups. These include psalms to be sung along with vocal parts for the presider and/or cantor.

This ancient form of prayer is so appropriate for us today, because the Liturgy of the Hours confronts our modern lack of time; it helps us recognize and prioritize our use of that sacred gift, time.

▶ *"At our parish, whenever we have a speaker or hold a workshop we place the activity within Morning Prayer and/or Evening Prayer. Then the entire event becomes a prayer experience."*

▶ *"When I preside for Morning Prayer I feel connected to peoples everywhere, even those predating history. How easy to imagine them gathering in the morning, to thank whatever gods may be, that they have been preserved through the night and the sun has been sent yet again to make its journey across the skies. While we have progressed in our scientific knowledge, we still need to rekindle some of that simplicity of faith and gratitude."*

▶ *"When I first left the convent I was aware of how much I missed my friends in the order. But now, so many years later, I find that I still miss the Liturgy of the Hours, when we prayed and sang as a community— and our only audience was God."*

▶ *"I always experience a sense of awe when I preside. Leading the community in prayer is both humbling and exhilarating! But I am especially affected by Evening Prayer. We always begin in semidarkness, so when I light the altar candles after the greeting I feel linked to people generations ago who had no choice but to endure the darkness of night. Those courageous, faithful people handed down their faith to us today."*

Word-Communion Liturgies

Because of the shortage of priests, there is an upsurge in the occurrence of Word-Communion services. However, the increasing frequency of this rite is not without its justified critics. Without presenting here a detailed

PRAYER
PREPARATION
PRACTICE
PRAYER

CONSIDER

What is the tradition in your parish community concerning the liturgy celebrated when a priest is not presiding?

What is the response to a Word-Communion service in your faith community?

When and where are Word-Communion services celebrated in your area? What is the response?

What is your response to celebrating the Liturgy of the Hours in place of the Word-Communion service?

How do you feel about being Eucharist for one another? Why?

explanation of the various positions taken by liturgists and theologians concerning the use of a Word-Communion service, the presider should be aware of the main points of controversy.

At first glance, a Word-Communion liturgy may not appear to differ significantly from a eucharistic liturgy. A general outline of a full Word-Communion liturgy includes:

INTRODUCTORY RITES
- Greeting
- Penitential Rite
- Opening Prayer

LITURGY OF THE WORD
- First Reading
- Responsorial Psalm
- Second Reading (if designated)
- Gospel Acclamation
- Gospel
- Sermon
- Intercessions

COMMUNION RITE
- Lord's Prayer
- Sign of Peace
- Invitation to Communion
- Communion
- Prayer After Communion
- Blessing
- Dismissal

Not all the above elements are always included in a Word-Communion service. For instance, the readings may be shortened or the prayer after communion omitted or other variations may be adopted. There would, of course, be music as well. The assembly becomes intimately involved in the service when it sings the responsorial psalm, the gospel acclamation, an opening hymn, a communion song and a closing hymn.

When all the above are included, however, the question remains: How does this differ from a eucharistic liturgy? To answer that question, we need to understand what Eucharist is. Eucharist is not that plastic-looking host; Eucharist is not even that bread-resembling substantial element. Eucharist is not a thing! Eucharist is an act—or more distinctly, a series of acts. Eucharist is the totality of the acts of gathering, of story-telling, of bread-breaking, of commissioning.

Within this framework of breaking bread, we who are the Body of Christ consecrate. We, the assembly, are necessary for Eucharist, for the priest is not even allowed to celebrate the eucharistic liturgy alone. The priest cannot do our work—liturgy—for us! Therefore, when we, in the absence of a priest-presider, celebrate a Word-Communion service using preconsecrated bread, we omit an essential part of the liturgy. A Word-Communion service is not the same as a eucharistic liturgy.

Many theologians and liturgists believe that a different liturgy should be celebrated when a priest is not presiding. They would suggest that the Liturgy of the Hours be used, with no distribution of Communion. Thus many theologians and liturgists would suggest Morning Prayer or Evening Prayer in place of a Word-Communion service. Morning or

Evening Prayer has an integrity of its own and can unquestionably be lead by a lay presider. Its main focus is the praise of God. Because it has long been part of our tradition it unites us with the entire Church.

Because we are a sacramental people, we need, desire and are entitled to the full sacrament of Eucharist. Be we also recognize the variety of ways in which the sacredness and sacramentality of life are presented to us. When we gather, when we celebrate the word of the Lord, when we praise our God, we are Eucharist for one another, nourishing one another with our presence.

▶ *"In our neighboring parish, whenever the pastor is on vacation or out of town he tells the people to attend daily liturgy at our church. Of course they are welcome to worship with us, but shouldn't that assembly gather at their own parish for liturgy? Isn't that what community means?"*

Children's Liturgies

When the priest performed the rituals of the Mass with his back to the congregation and recited the prayers in Latin, many adults didn't fully understand what was going on, so they weren't disturbed that children in the congregation didn't understand. Since Vatican II, we've come to recognize our essential part as the main minister of the liturgy. We need to understand what we are doing, and we want our children to understand, appreciate and participate in our liturgies as well.

Our main weekend liturgies are to include children and youth as essential members of the assembly. While a faith community is not to have a special children's eucharistic liturgy on Sunday, all of us have responsibilities toward the young.

We are to express hospitality to children and youth, recognizing them as full members of the community. Children, no less than adults, can experience God in their own way; they have an innate spiritual essence. We cherish children, recognizing that they are the product of both human and divine love, the promise of hope, the bearers of faith into the future.

All the faith community have responsibilities to the youth of the community and of the world. But those of us who preside at children's liturgies are especially privileged. We are able to touch the future through the young with whom we pray. As adults in the community, we offer to the young examples of mature faith. We need to acknowledge and accept the responsibility of being spiritual mentors for the young. We demonstrate for children the art of public worship.

While the faith community would ordinarily not have a special weekend liturgy for children, lay presiders often have ample opportunities to celebrate children's liturgies. These might include a separate Sunday Liturgy of the Word, parish school or religious education classes, children's retreats or impromptu rituals.

The young offer so much to us, the adults who work with them. We adults need to listen to them, remain open to them and to what the Holy Spirit may be teaching us through the young.

Presiding for children's liturgies requires the same qualities needed for the liturgies of the faith community. There are, of course, some additional points to remember when presiding with children. Avoid patronizing them; children are sensitive to such treatment. Do not belittle

CONSIDER

How are children welcomed to the liturgies of your faith community? Could this be improved? How?

What provisions are made in your worship space for babies and young children? Could these be improved? How?

How are children involved in your regular weekend liturgies? In special liturgies?

How do the religious education programs prepare children for the weekend liturgies?

How are young people encouraged to participate in your liturgies? What improvements could be made?

What do you most enjoy about working with children? Why?

What do you want to accomplish while presiding for a children's liturgy? Why?

What is different about presiding for a children's liturgy and a liturgy of the larger faith community?

What concerns do you have about presiding for a children's liturgy? How can you deal with these concerns?

What unique gifts and talents do you bring to this ministry?

The Christian communities to which the individual families belong or in which the children live also have a responsibility toward children baptized in the Church. By giving witness to the Gospel, living communal charity, and actively celebrating the mysteries of Christ, the Christian community is an excellent school of Christian and liturgical formation for the children who live in it. (Directory for Masses With Children, #11)

In many places parish Masses are celebrated, especially on Sundays and holy days, at which a good many children take part along with the large number of adults. On such occasions the witness of adult believers can have a great effect upon the children. Adults can in turn benefit spiritually from experiencing the part that the children have within the Christian community. The Christian spirit of the family is greatly fostered when children take part in these Masses together with their parents and other family members. (Directory for Masses With Children, #16)

their experiences of the divine. God does not operate an adults-only business. Take children's questions seriously, for what seems trivial to us may have extreme importance to them. Distinguish between being childish and being childlike.

Avoid being preachy. We need to remember that we are not God; we should never be afraid to reveal that we don't have all the answers. Emphasize that there is always more to learn and comprehend about faith, God, relationships, worship and Scripture. Present children with a God and a faith that can survive the harsh reality that many have already experienced in life.

Recognize that children know how to pray with their bodies. Just as they play and learn with their entire being, so too they pray with their entire being. Encourage imagination and creativity in all areas, including prayer, God-images and the human-divine relationship. Incorporate good and tasteful art, music, literature and liturgical dance in liturgies; children deserve the best.

Present experiences of symbols and rituals, but do not try to explain and teach everything; children are often more open to symbols than are many adults. Be authentic and genuine in what you say and do. Children need the real thing and have an uncanny ability to detect impostors. If the faith that we present to the young is shallow, they shall soon grow out of it. So, above all, children's liturgies must be genuine, faith-filled experiences of public prayer.

Many resources are available for working with children's liturgy. In choosing materials to use with children, we seek books, ideas, programs and videos that honor the dignity of childhood and recognize the validity of childhood experiences, searchings or questionings. These materials should not limit or restrict a child's possible relationship with God nor a child's images of God. In addition, religious education programs should support community and public worship and provide a foundation for an adult relationship with God.

Perhaps the most important consideration in the choice of materials is that we need to be comfortable in what we do. If we are comfortable with the program and believe in its approach, then we will be both effective and sincere in our work. In our interaction with children we are providing them with the basis of their lifelong faith.

▶ *"Occasionally our pastor, at homily time, invites the grade-school children to come up on the sanctuary steps and gather around him. He then tells a story, perhaps even including the kids in the telling of it. While the story is for all of us, it's always one that kids can follow and understand. For me, even after I've forgotten the story, I can still picture Father surrounded by kids!"*

▶ *"I asked the kids to tell me what a saint is. One little boy, pointing to the stained glass window above him, answered, 'A saint is someone who lets the light shine through.' I thought about that for a moment, then agreed. 'Yes,' I answered. 'Being a saint means letting the light of Christ shine through us.'"*

▶ *"I conducted a retreat for ninety first-, second- and third-graders. Some of the other teachers were astonished when I used centering prayer with these kids, but Jesus did speak to them. Christ is present in the young!"*

Ministering to the Sick

Those who visit and minister to the sick, aged and hospitalized carry on a tradition rich in ritual. The ministering can take many forms: the lay pastoral caregiver or minister can pray with the individual and/or family, bring communion to the individual and caregivers, read Scripture for those gathered, tell an inspiring or humorous story, sing hymns or antiphons with those present, bless and/or anoint the individual and caregivers, recognize and encourage the gifts and talents of the hospitalized or homebound.

In visiting the ill the presider needs to incorporate ritual, music and Scripture; we all have a basic need for ritual, whether those rituals are part of the public worship of the community or part of the family experience around the bed of the infirm or the semiprivate interaction of the lay pastoral caregiver and the elderly. The lasting power of ritual remains with people as a gift of memories—memories of psalms, songs, blessings, anointings or other symbolic actions. Many of these ideas are listed elsewhere in this book.

Within our ministry we also have the opportunity to encourage the convalescent or elderly to use their gifts and talents. Many times we come to cheer or be supportive of the hospitalized or homebound, only to have them cheer and support us. In their pain and silence and inactivity, the ill and aged often are blessed with insight, courage and the love of God. They can extend these gifts to others. Many of those we visit have a rich and active prayer life; they can offer to the world the much-needed gift of their prayers.

A convenient handbook for lay presiders and pastoral caregivers is *A Ritual for Laypersons: Rites for Holy Communion and the Pastoral Care of the Sick and Dying*. It is a fine and inexpensive book, with contents collected from several sources, but it contains no background information or explanations; it assumes that the user is already familiar with the rites. Also, note that while this book is ideal for rituals held in a small intimate space, such as a sickroom, a larger book would be more appropriate for a rite in a chapel or church setting.

The pastoral caregiver is the community representative to those who cannot be part of the worshiping assembly. It is a privilege to bring the sacramental presence of Christ to those unable to attend the community's eucharistic celebrations.

During a visit to the hospital or nursing facility or sickroom, the pastoral minister can bring not only the gift of communion and the gift of presence, but also the gift of music. We may choose a hymn to be sung with or for the one we are visiting or perhaps a refrain from a psalm setting. We may also bring an appropriate piece of recorded music. The gift of music is a lasting one, for those we visit can recall it as often as desired. Through music we offer the person being visited—and the family and friends gathered there—an enduring and consoling memory.

▶ *"The pastoral minister who came every week to visit my mom always sang the twenty-third psalm, 'The Lord is my Shepherd,' to help her prepare for communion. Mom loved it! And, of course, that's what we sang at her funeral—it was just right!"*

▶ *"When I do my pastoral-care visits and bring communion, I always*

The blessing of the sick by the ministers of the Church is a very ancient custom, having its origins in the practice of Christ himself and his apostles. When ministers visit those who are sick, they are to respect the provisions of Pastoral Care of the Sick...but the primary concern of every minister should be to show the sick how much Christ and his Church are concerned for them. (Book of Blessings, #376) wonder if I am bringing holy viaticum—the last communion—to one of them. Perhaps that communion is to be that person's food for the greatest journey."

CONSIDER

What does the Paschal Mystery mean to you? What effect does it have in your everyday life?

What are some of the milestones near the end of life that our society celebrates? Some that our society ignores?

If you could choose another sacrament to add to the present seven, what would it be?

How did you first become involved in this ministry? Why do you continue your involvement?

What particular talents or gifts do you bring to this ministry?

What personal experiences of death could have been made more bearable with the aid of a pastoral minister?

When has a pastoral minister effectively ministered to you?

What rituals or symbols do you include in your visits to the homebound and the dying?

How can you choose rituals or symbols that help both the dying person and the family?

How do you benefit from this ministry?

Ministering to the Dying

We recognize, honor, ritualize, celebrate the events surrounding the beginning of life: pregnancy, birth, baptism, the many "firsts" of an individual's coming into the fullness of being. No less worthy of recognition are the "lasts" of life: limitations caused by age or terminal illness, the approach of death, death itself, the good-byes of family and friends, the funeral, the committal or burial. These too deserve to be ritualized for they most eloquently testify to our faith. All aspects of these end times are filled with opportunities of ritualized ministry to the individual, the mourning family, the grieving community.

The pastoral caregiver and presider can help the community not only get through this traumatic time, but discover within it courage, hope, new awakenings and an enriched fullness of community. To do this requires that those involved be sensitive to and knowledgeable about the Catholic theology of death and resurrection, emotionally able to console others and personally open to the Holy Spirit, who so often speaks through the experiences of others.

"Companions on a journey," "pilgrim people"—how often community is symbolized as travel or a journey. Then the metaphor for death is the earthly end point of a pilgrim. Those who minister to the dying and their families have an extremely demanding yet satisfying and inspiring ministry. They walk together in strained hope, in questioning faith and in flawed love with those most in need of companionship. When death is the near destination, then the Church as a pilgrim people marches along, sometimes walking beside those in need, sometimes carrying both the needy and their burdens.

This ministry is an integral element of Christian community. The presider comes to the dying and their families as a representative of the faith community. We serve them as we serve the ill; here, however, the hope may no longer be for bodily health, but for the healing that can accompany the Christian into eternity.

Even when the ill person is unable to speak or has difficulty receiving communion, we can still minister through the sense of touch. We can make the Sign of the Cross on the person's forehead or in the palm of the hand; we can rub the person's feet or back; we can stroke the person's hair. However we minister, it is done with consideration for all and with their approval.

All these actions acknowledge our presence and convey our care. They can be accompanied by prayer, Scripture and song. In instances of a long disability or terminal illness, these actions become rituals of great meaning to the individual and family; they are symbols of a caring Church.

▶ *"Mark, the lay pastoral caregiver who visited my dad in his last illness, was wonderful. Every time he brought communion to Dad he conducted a short service: a Scripture reading, a prayer, a hymn. Often he sang a psalm and the family, including my dad when he was able, joined in on*

"If one member suffers in the body of Christ which is the Church, all the members suffer with that member" (1 Corinthians 12:26). *For this reason, those who are baptized into Christ and nourished at the same table of the Lord are responsible for one another. When Christians are sick, their brothers and sisters share a ministry of mutual charity and "do all that they can to help the sick return to health, by showing love for the sick, and by celebrating the sacraments with them."* (Order of Christian Funerals, #8)

CONSIDER

What is the tradition in your parish concerning vigils and wakes? How do they compare with those in the *Order of Christian Funerals*?

Is the family usually involved in the planning of the endtime rituals and liturgies? Is the family usually involved in the actual rituals and liturgies?

What is the tradition at your parish concerning music at vigil, funeral and committal services? Is there anything that needs to be done to improve the role of music in these liturgies? If yes, what is your part in this?

What do you consider the greatest challenge to presiding for these endtime liturgies? How do you plan to deal with this?

What special gifts or talents do you bring to this ministry?

Who usually presides at committal services? Pastor? Associate pastor? Deacon? Lay presider? Someone from the funeral home? A family member?

How do you feel about presiding at committal services? Why?

How prepared are you to preside for a

the refrain. When Dad died, Mark came to the house and the family gathered and prayed for one last time around the bed where Dad lay. When the mortician arrived, we accompanied Dad's body from the bedroom and processed out, with Mark leading the singing. That special time, immediately following Dad's death, was our family's private good-bye to him."

▶ *"My mom was a hugger! She loved to hug us kids, her friends, and as for her grandkids—they learned early what it meant to be really hugged! So it was an extra cross for her, and indirectly for us, that when she was dying she couldn't bear to be touched! No more hugging. But when Nadine brought communion to Mom and visited with her, before leaving, Nadine would put her arms around herself and give herself two hugs, announcing that one was from Mom and the other was for Mom."*

Ministering to the Mourning

The presider is the representative of the faith community to the mourning family. In the name of that faith community we can be with them at the time of the loved one's death and the removal of the body from the home, hospice or hospital. We can be with them during the preparation of the body and the family's first viewing of the body. We can be with them through the visitation, the vigil service, the funeral, the committal or graveside service and the community's farewell meal. We can also be with them throughout the period of mourning.

The presider's involvement in the rituals following death is determined by consideration of the family's wishes, including those of the deceased, the customs of the faith community, the ethnic and personal traditions of the family and finally our own commitments.

As presiders, we recognize that the main comfort to the mourners comes not from us, but from the consoling familiarity of the various rites and music and Scripture; the comfort comes from the presence of the community. The presider's role is to encourage the community to reach out to the grieving and surround them with love and support.

Whether we are dealing with the terminal illness of an aged member of the community, the sudden death of an infant or the accidental death of a young father, we must try to balance the tensions inherent in the situation: our joyful belief in the resurrection and the agonizing grief and sorrow of those who mourn; our belief in a loving God and our unanswered questions about life and death; our celebration of the liturgical season or feast and our celebration of this particular vigil or funeral; our celebration of life and our celebration of death; our responsibilities to those who mourn and our responsibilities to the faith community.

In balancing our pastoral sensitivity to the mourners and our responsibilities to the liturgy and our faith tradition, we need to avoid two extremes: One is to plan a "generic" funeral that is completely impersonal; the other is to plan a funeral so personalized that the rite itself is diminished.

Generic vigils and funerals offer no recognition of the life of this individual, this loved one. On the other hand, the funeral rites are public expressions of the faith community's beliefs about worship, life and

committal or burial service? A vigil? A funeral?

How familiar are you with the *Order of Christian Funerals*? With the variations and options available?

What are three main thoughts that would be appropriate to offer to those who mourn?

How do such liturgies affect you personally?

What special talents, insights, experiences do you bring to this ministry?

Members of the local parish community should be encouraged to participate in the vigil as a sign of concern and support for the mourners.... The vigil may also serve as an opportunity for participation in the funeral by those who, because of work or other reasons, cannot be present for the funeral liturgy or the rite of committal. (Order of Christian Funerals, #64)

The liturgical color chosen for funerals should express Christian hope but should not be offensive to human grief or sorrow. In the United States, white, violet, or black vestments may be worn at the funeral rites and at other offices and Masses for the dead. (Order of Christian Funerals, #39)

death. Personalizing these services and rituals must be theologically and liturgically acceptable. Guidelines for environment, music, liturgical dance, liturgical language and vesture still apply.

As presiders we need to be even more hospitable than usual at these endtime liturgies and rites. Both the presider and the community need to be sensitive to the trauma of those who remain and their need for healing. We need to be attentive to the wishes of the deceased, as well as to the culture and traditions of the deceased, the family and the faith community. We need to be aware of the presence of non-Catholics, non-churchgoers and Catholics who have not been active recently in the Church. Above all we need to remember the Holy Spirit's presence working through such human events.

The *Order of Christian Funerals* offers wonderful suggestions concerning options for services (including Morning or Evening Prayer), poignant prayers and intercessions, and suggestions for appropriate music and Scripture texts.

The *Order of Christian Funerals* also offers guidelines concerning eulogies. This tradition of offering personal assurances to the family that the deceased will not be forgotten is part of the grief-healing process. This must, however, take its proper place in the rite.

Occasionally the family may request readings and music that are not in line with liturgical standards and practices for a eucharistic liturgy. They may, however, be acceptable in either the vigil or committal service. The funeral vigil, for example, offers opportunities to include the sharing of remembrances, the singing of favorite hymns and songs, the reading of a much-loved meditation or poem, a memorabilia table, the displaying of crafts or works of art of the deceased.

If the lay pastoral caregiver is not the presider for the funeral, that person may preside for the vigil or the committal service. Or, the pastoral minister may serve in another capacity, such as eucharistic minister or lector, thus linking together the ministries of the faith community.

It is important for family members to be involved in the planning of these liturgies and rituals; it can be especially consoling to have the offspring, such as grandchildren of the deceased, involved in the rites, for the presence of children at a funeral is itself a reminder of the Paschal Mystery. Working out the details and assessing the ability of those to be involved during this traumatic time requires the pastoral sensitivity of the parish staff, the pastoral caregivers and presiders.

In some instances a community may decide to celebrate a memorial service, possibly using the Morning Prayer or Evening Prayer format. A memorial service celebrating the life of the deceased may be the appropriate choice when the funeral liturgy is celebrated elsewhere or when the body of the deceased is not present (as when it has been donated to scientific causes).

It is important to schedule the funeral services so that the community can attend. For example, evening services can accommodate people who have other commitments during the day. This allows the family to be surrounded by the support of their whole community. The gathering of the community witnesses to an eventual heavenly reunion of all in God's love.

The symbols utilized in the funeral liturgies include the symbols of Baptism (water, white garment or pall, candles), the symbols of Easter and resurrection (a cross, the paschal candle, fresh flowers), the symbols

Music is integral to the funeral rites. It allows the community to express convictions and feelings that words alone may fail to convey. It has the power to console and uplift the mourners and to strengthen the unity of the assembly in faith and love. The texts of the songs chosen for a particular celebration should express the paschal mystery of the Lord's suffering, death, and triumph over death and should be related to the readings from Scripture. (Order of Christian Funerals #30)

The singing of well-chosen music at the rite of committal can help the mourners as they face the reality of the separation. At the rite of committal with final commendation, whenever possible, the song of farewell should be sung. In either form of the committal rite, a hymn or liturgical song that affirms hope in God's mercy and in the resurrection of the dead is desirable at the conclusion of the rite. (Order of Christian Funerals, #214)

So too when a member of Christ's Body dies, the faithful are called to a ministry of consolation to those who have suffered the loss of one whom they love. Christian consolation is rooted in that hope that comes from faith in the saving death and resurrection of the Lord Jesus Christ. Christian hope faces the reality of death and the anguish of grief but trusts confidently that the power of sin and death has been vanquished by the risen Lord. The Church calls each member of Christ's Body—priest, deacon, layperson—to participate in the ministry of consolation: to care for the dying, to pray for the dead, to comfort those who mourn. (Order of Christian Funerals, #8)

The vigil for the deceased is the principal rite celebrated by the Christian community in the time following death and before the funeral liturgy, or if there is no funeral liturgy, before the rite of committal. It may take the form either of a liturgy of the word or of some part of the office for the dead [i.e., Morning or Evening Prayer]. (Order of Christian Funerals, #54)

of Christian life (Bible, incense). Special efforts should be made to include music in the rituals and liturgies that mark the death of a member.

While music is traditionally included in the funeral liturgy itself, it is also recommended that music be a part of the vigil service and committal or burial service also. The people involved in the presiding and music ministries need to work together to achieve this goal. A faith community's attending to just one or two tasks may make this possible.

For example, the community may want to assemble a booklet containing music for vigils and committal services and/or a booklet containing music and rituals for lay pastoral caregivers. The music for a committal or burial service needs to be familiar to the people, easy to sing and appropriate to the situation. The words and/or music for this service can be included in the funeral worship aid or booklet.

The community may also want to provide some training in music for presiders and lay pastoral caregivers. Well-known hymns need but a start by the presider or a member of the assembly and people will join in the singing. Other options include having a cantor accompanied by guitar, flute, oboe or trumpet. Consulting with the music director or liturgical musician will probably reveal other workable solutions.

The first choice in planning should include singing by the assembly. Practical considerations need to be considered, however, such as size of the gathering and emotional state of the mourners. And, of course, the weather conditions of the moment can instantly disrupt the most careful planning.

The task of presiding for the committal service often comes to lay presiders since pastors may lack the necessary time. Although many mortuaries provide this service, it is much more fitting that this grace-filled ritual of Christian love be conducted by a member of the faith community.

Everything about the death of a close friend or family member is painful and difficult. The flurry of necessary activity immediately following death, however, often prevents the survivors from confronting its permanence. The burial or committal service at the cemetery has a finality about it that can be emotionally devastating. The faith community, in its walk with the mourners on their journey, is present here too.

Because the presider usually does not have much preparation time before a funeral, it is necessary to do the groundwork well in advance. We familiarize ourselves with the basic rites and possible variations. In this way we will be able to preside well, to minister to the mourners, to serve the liturgy, to assist the community in walking with those who mourn, and to be transparent so that those present can see beyond us to the goodness and mercy of God.

▶ *"The funeral of my friend's mother was held at a small old church that had its own cemetery on the property. At the conclusion of the eucharistic liturgy we processed, singing, to the burial site for the committal ritual, as the pallbearers carried the coffin. It was all of a piece, the funeral and burial, and it had an integrity that I had never before recognized."*

▶ *"I always wondered how non-Catholics felt when they came to a service at a funeral home and we said the rosary. The vigil service, with*

The full participation by all present is to be encouraged. This is best achieved through careful planning of the celebration. Whenever possible, the family of the deceased should take part in the selection of texts and music and in the designation of liturgical ministers. (Order of Christian Funerals, #65)

The rite of committal, the conclusion of the funeral rites, is the final act of the community of faith in caring for the body of its deceased member. It may be celebrated at the grave, tomb, or crematorium and may be used for burial at sea.... The rite of committal is an expression of the communion that exists between the Church on earth and the Church in heaven. (Order of Christian Funerals, #204, 206)

Funeral rites are to be granted to those who have chosen cremation, unless there is evidence that their choice was dictated by anti-Christian motives. The funeral is to be celebrated according to the model in use in the region.... The rites usually held in the cemetery chapel or at the grave may in this case take place within the confines of the crematorium.... Every precaution is to be taken against the danger of scandal or religious indifferentism. (Appendix, Order of Christian Funerals, #15)

Scripture readings and singing by the assembly, seems so much more hospitable to all who come."

▶ *"Sometimes when I meet with the family of the deceased to plan the funeral and vigil they come with a long list of favorite songs. I have to remind them that we are not planning a concert or a hymn-sing, but a community liturgy."*

▶ *"At our parish it no longer matters if there are to be many or few people attending a funeral—we always print a worship aid. The liturgy board decided that having a worship aid was one way for the faith community to recognize the importance of that person's life. And so, there are worship aids for all funerals, large or small. Surely that is not too much to do!"*

▶ *"Tom's widow asked my husband and me to help with the vigil service. After an opening hymn, I welcomed the people to our parish, told some stories about Tom, and then invited others to contribute their own word pictures. At the appropriate time, my husband concluded the reminiscences by telling about Tom's love for a particular hymn. Singing the hymn then moved us into the rest of the service."*

▶ *"How I dreaded my mother's funeral. But the liturgist involved our family in both the planning of the funeral and in the liturgy itself. The befriender who had been visiting Mom read the Scripture texts that Mom had picked out herself. We sang some of Mom's favorite hymns, including the one that the befriender sang when she brought communion. A friend, who is a lay presider, did the graveside service. It was tremendously consoling to have someone who actually knew our family help us say that final goodbye to Mom. I never thought I'd be saying this, but Mom's funeral was really beautiful."*

▶ *"I have danced in the cathedral at chrism masses and ordinations; I have danced in my parish church at Christmas and Triduum. When my father died, what could be more meaningful to me than to dance at my father's funeral? As I led the congregation in the gestures of the offertory refrain, I felt at peace with his death—and I knew he was pleased with my dancing."*

▶ *"I presided for the committal service for Jim's wife, who loved roses. Since Jim's roses were in bloom, the morning of the funeral I harvested a large bowl of petals from his garden. At the cemetery I also had available another bowl filled with water, which we all blessed. Following the closing hymn, I invited the friends and family to say their final good-bye using either or both the water and the roses. I believe people need to make some last gesture of farewell and I consider it part of my task as presider to offer them the opportunity to do so."*

▶ *"When I began presiding and was faced with doing a committal service I did some fast preparation! Afterward, as I spent more time with the* Order of Christian Funerals *book, I was amazed at how narrow and limited is our usual celebration of funerals. The funeral rites most certainly have not yet been fully explored."*

Sunday Celebrations in the Absence of a Priest

We begin with an immediate need for clarification. Christians can gather at any time and on any day to praise God in public worship. As Jesus told his disciples, "[W]here two or three are gathered in my name, I am there among them" (Matthew 18:20). Any gathering of Christians is the Church. Morning Prayer or Evening Prayer, for example, or another service, may be held on any day of the week, including Sunday.

The Sunday Celebration in the Absence of a Priest is a specific set of rites detailed in a rite book entitled *Sunday Celebrations in the Absence of a Priest*. This book contains much valuable information: recognition of the importance of the gathering of the community; background about the Christian celebration of the Lord's Day; the significant differences in celebrating any liturgy that is not a full eucharistic liturgy; emphasis on the assembly's right and need to hear proclaimed the word of God for each specific Sunday; role of the deacon in such instances; assurance that attendance at a Sunday Celebration in the Absence of a Priest does fulfill the Sunday obligation; the guidelines concerning the use of this rite.

In some localities this rite is to be used only in the most extreme emergencies. In other locations it may be routinely scheduled because there is no other option. Anyone who might be called upon to preside for this rite should be aware of the local bishop's ruling.

The variations of this service are described in the rite book. It should be noted that the order of this service differs from the more flexible Word-Communion service. A Word-Communion service is a general form that can be quite varied; for example, the simple act of bringing Communion to the homebound and reading a Scripture text can be described as a Word-Communion service.

The rite book also spells out the role of music in this liturgy. Since this would be celebrated in place of the usual Sunday eucharistic liturgy, it is assumed that the involvement of the choir, musicians, cantors and assembly would be similar.

A commissioning service of the lay presider for this rite should be considered. This commissioning could emphasize the diocesan approval of the implementation of the Sunday Celebration in the Absence of a Priest, the choice of the lay presider and the concurrence of the assembly, whose work the liturgy is.

▶ *"During a family trip we stopped at a small town for Sunday Mass. It happened that the pastor of this one-priest parish had become ill during the night and was unable to preside. So several laypeople and the organist/music director got together and did a service. My family and I were quite overwhelmed by this community's closeness and prayerfulness, along with their concern for their pastor. This happened a number of years ago—but I've never forgotten it."*

Rite of Christian Initiation of Adults

The Second Vatican Council presented to the community an incredibly beautiful jewel in the process called the Rite of Christian Initiation of Adults (RCIA). This is not a program of lectures, delivered by the parish staff, about doctrines and dogmas; this is faith-sharing by members of the

CONSIDER

How do you feel about a Sunday celebration without an ordained priest presiding? What do you see lacking?

Which do you prefer: Morning/Evening Prayer or the Sunday Celebration in the Absence of a Priest? Why?

How would you feel about presiding for a Sunday Celebration in the Absence of a Priest? Why?

What plans are in place in your faith community for music at a Sunday Celebration in the Absence of a Priest? How do these plans compare with the usual Sunday liturgy with a priest presiding? Is there a difference? Why?

Bible services should be encouraged, especially on the vigils of the more solemn feasts, on some weekdays in Advent and Lent, and on Sundays and holy days. They are particularly to be recommended in places where no priest is available; when this is the case, a deacon or some other person authorized by the bishop is to preside over the celebration. (Constitution on the Sacred Liturgy, #35:4)

CONSIDER

How does teaching prospective new members about doctrine and dogma differ from telling them personal faith stories? What are the advantages of each method? The disadvantages?

What is your understanding of the Rite of Christian Initiation of Adults? What is your experience of it? When does your parish community experience the Rite of Christian Initiation of Adults? How can this experience be deepened?

The Christian initiation process involves rites and rituals. What does this say about the importance of such traditions within our faith life?

Catechists, who have an important office for the progress of the catechumens and for the growth of the community, should, whenever possible, have an active part in the rites. When deputed by the bishop (see no. 12), they may perform the minor exorcism and blessings contained in the ritual. (Rite of Christian Initiation of Adults, #16)

CONSIDER

What is the likelihood of your being called to perform an emergency baptism for someone in danger of death? Why?

As a lay presider might you be considered by your faith community as a logical choice to baptize in an emergency?

Are you prepared to perform an emergency baptism? If not, what do you need to do to prepare yourself?

In imminent danger of death and especially at the moment of death, when no priest or deacon is available, any mem-

community. Christian initiation involves not just the members of the initiation team, but the entire faith community.

As we believers pass on our faith to these new members, we are renewed in that faith. As we speak of our beliefs and our doubts, of our mountaintop experiences and our wanderings in the deserts of our times of nearness to God and our times of seeming estrangement from God, of our understanding of the gospel and our whisperings of the Holy Spirit, we are ourselves rejuvenated.

This process validates our own experiences as the People of God. Throughout the liturgical year the Sunday liturgy incorporates rites recognizing those going through Christian Initiation, the candidates and the catechumens. We, the faith community, welcome them, pray for them, commit ourselves to support them and to walk with them in their journey. The initiation of adults is the responsibility of all the baptized.

The initiation process also includes many "minor rites" such as blessings and anointings that can be celebrated by catechists and other laypeople on the initiation team. Those who perform these rites need to be familiar with the presiding role and with the skills involved in a meaningful celebration of the rites.

▶ *"I've been on our parish's RCIA core team for several years. It is tremendously encouraging to me to see how, each year, former candidates and catechumens make special efforts to attend the rites for the current initiates. They always join us in the celebrations afterwards, and are so supportive of everyone involved in the RCIA. These people understand what it means to be active in the faith community!"*

▶ *"During the RCIA's Rite of Welcoming I am really moved as I watch the sponsors signing the senses of our potential new members. Having lay people do that brings home to me that we, the whole community, are the ones who walk in faith with the candidates and catechumens."*

Baptism

No matter what accomplishment or recognition we can claim throughout our entire life—even ordination—nothing is as significant to our being as baptism. This initiation into the Christian faith is worthy of the highest degree of celebration. It is a sacred commitment on the part of the individual and on the part of the welcoming community. The process of moving from the unbaptized state to joining the ranks of the believing community is a truly momentous event!

This welcoming is to be celebrated with greatest solemnity and joy. For the newborn and very young, therefore, the baptism ideally takes place during a Sunday liturgy, with the faith community witnessing and taking part in the celebration.

Adults who have participated in the Rite of Christian Initiation of Adults and have been guided in the faith journey by members of the community are baptized at the most solemn, joyous and spectacular liturgy of the entire year: the Easter Vigil. That fact in itself indicates with what ceremony the event is to be surrounded.

Life is not always predictable, however; death, or the threat of death, can interrupt the most laudable plans. Therefore provisions exist for the

ber of the faithful, indeed anyone with the right intention, may and sometimes must administer baptism. In a case simply of danger of death the sacrament should be administered, if possible, by a member of the faithful according to one of the shorter rites provided for this situation. Even in this case a small community should be formed to assist at the rite or, if possible, at least one or two witnesses should be present. (Rite of Baptism, #16)

Since they belong to the priestly people, all laypersons, especially parents and, by reason of their work, catechists, midwives, family or social workers or nurses of the sick, as well as physicians and surgeons, should be thoroughly aware, according to their capacities, of the proper methods of baptizing in case of emergency. They should be taught by pastors, deacons, and catechists. Bishops should provide appropriate means within their diocese for such instruction. (Rite of Baptism, #17)

CONSIDER

As a member of the assembly, what liturgical adaptions have you experienced that added to the liturgy? How did they make the liturgy more meaningful for you?

As a member of the assembly, what liturgical adaptions have you experienced that detracted from the liturgy? How did they make the liturgy less meaningful for you?

What do you see as the most persuasive reasons for making liturgical adaptations?

Who in your faith community or on the parish staff can you consult for assistance in making adaptations?

What stories do you know where lack of sensitivity to another caused much pain

unbaptized who are in danger of death. Contained in the Rites of Christian Initiation are the various forms for the baptism rituals. These forms range from the most formal and ritualized rites (such as the baptisms within the Easter Vigil or the Sunday liturgy) to the simplest form to be used only in emergency.

Under ordinary circumstances, baptism is performed by a priest or a deacon. But when the person to be baptized is in danger of death, much of the formal ritual is laid aside. The details of the rites are explained in these two sections of the book: "Rite of Baptism for Children in Danger of Death When No Priest or Deacon is Available" (#157) and "Christian Initiation of a Person in Danger of Death" (#375).

When there is time for some ritual recognition of the magnitude of the sacrament, these should be included, as explained in the above references. However, the emergency form is presented here.

The basic baptismal rite, which may be done using ordinary water, is as follows.

The layperson baptizes the individual, using the person's name, saying:

> (NAME), I baptize you in the name of the Father (pours water on the head of the person the first time), and of the Son (pours water the second time), and of the Holy Spirit (pours water the third time).

This omission of all extra ritual and ceremony is to be done only in extreme emergency. In addition, the lay person should have, if possible, one or more witnesses to the baptism.

Pastoral Adaptations

In many documents and directives from the Second Vatican Council or the National Conference of Catholic Bishops or some other authority, after the goals and guidelines are enumerated there is mention of pastoral concerns. This allows the local bishop, if he deems it wise or compassionate, to adapt the directives before sending them on to the individual pastors. This allows the individual pastor, if he deems it prudent, to adapt the directives for a specific faith community.

The reason for these changes is pastoral, that is, meeting the individual needs of people today. Being pastoral means being sensitive to people—to all of us. It means being caught up in the spirit of the law rather than being obsessed with the letter of that law. Being pastoral means we, as presiders, are open, vulnerable and united with the community. We know each other's pain and brokenness, dreams and nightmares; we recognize the differences in our faith journeys; we admit both our inspiring faithfulness to love and our chasms of doubt and failure.

Being a pastoral presider means recognizing the difference between a funeral vigil for an eighty-nine-year-old great-grandpa and that of a six-year-old killed by a drunk driver. It means recognizing that our own personal choice in music or art or ritual may not speak to everyone else. As pastoral presiders we respond to the areas of sensitivity in others. We remember that faith and theology are not static, and we recognize teachable moments as we interact with others. We are sensitive to the

or misunderstanding? What would you, having 20/20 hindsight, now offer as a better solution?

What are some situations requiring pastoral judgment that you might encounter as a presider? What guidelines would you use in those situations?

How can you become better prepared to be a pastoral presider?

In planning and carrying out the funeral rites the pastor and all other ministers should keep in mind the life of the deceased and the circumstances of death. They should also take into consideration the spiritual and psychological needs of the family and friends of the deceased to express grief and their sense of loss, to accept the reality of death, and to comfort one another. (Order of Christian Funerals, #16)

traumas others experience. We recognize that others have not had our experience, and that we have not had the experiences of others.

Being pastoral affirms that the Church is people. Being pastoral, however, does not mean we do anything we want! Nor does it mean that we as presiders are to do everything anyone else requests of us. We need to maintain a balance between the extremes of ritual purists and pastoral purists. We, and those with whom we celebrate ritual and liturgy, must come to terms with what being Catholic means.

Liturgy is liturgy; it is not free-form worship. Catholic liturgy and ritual speak of our beliefs and reflect our images of God and of humanity. Catholic liturgy makes statements of our faith community and connects us with the greater Church. Catholic liturgy is the work of the people. As presiders in our faith community, we have responsibilities. These include serving the assembly and the community hospitably, honoring and respecting the liturgy, being faithful to who we are, upholding our Christian/Catholic faith and tradition, being open to the Holy Spirit and worshiping and honoring God reverently.

Maintaining an openness to the Holy Spirit is essential if the presider is to keep all these commitments in balance in a pastoral manner. A presider will be confronted with situations that demand adaptations of the rites. We need to know how to go about making such presiding revisions. What is allowed? What is appropriate?

Familiarity with the rites assures us that there are many places for individual choices or adaptation because of pastoral considerations. We need to acquire this familiarity; our basic need as presiders is to understand, experience, feel the rites as they are intended to be. We need to be attuned to the rite, grasp its theology, respond to its affectivity, be familiar with how it works and how it is envisioned. Such insight helps establish the ground rules of the rite or ritual, enabling us to appreciate both its value and its intent.

In the meantime, as we begin presiding we need to concentrate on performing our own role well. Summarizing much of the previous material, this means maintaining an active prayer life, presiding hospitably, reading and praying well, authentically proclaiming the word of God, choosing liturgically appropriate music and art, maintaining a high standard for lay presiding, being authentic to the assembly, being transparent in our presiding, being willing to be transformed by the liturgy and by presiding, being willing to learn and study.

Attending to these goals helps develop standards with which to deal with adaptations. Some liturgies, by their very nature, call for personalization: funerals and funeral vigils and committal or burial services, children's liturgies, healing services and others.

Changes or adaptations to the liturgy are made for pastoral reasons but do not detract from the liturgy itself. Some additional guidelines in adapting a liturgy are that the changes or adaptations add to both the hospitality and reverence of the liturgy, are prayerfully done, increase the involvement of the assembly, increase focus on the liturgy or the ritual rather than the ministers. Because we both love and respect liturgy, we weigh carefully any changes or adaptations.

▶ *"I've been a church organist for many years! I remember accompanying the singing of the* Dies Irae *at funerals. Then came the transition time when we first began singing in English. We took one look at the translation: 'That day of wrath, that dreadful day, Shall heaven and earth in ashes lay....' and we never sang it in English!"*

▶ *"The story of my grandmother's death has been told for many years in our family. With absolutely no warning my grandmother died at the age of thirty-eight, leaving my grandfather with four young children to raise. He was devastated! Fighting shock, Grandpa went to the pastor to arrange for the funeral. The priest informed him there was an extra charge to toll the bell; Grandpa did not have the money. My grandmother was buried without the tolling of the bell—and Grandpa never again entered a church."*

Private Piety

Presiders are to be people of prayer. So, while it seems difficult to imagine that we can overdo praying, we do recognize that prayer can be misused. We, as presiders, are in a position to dominate others, confuse them or to instruct them incorrectly about our faith and its practices.

As each of us responds to our baptismal call we do so in ways that recognize our individual personality, talents and gifts. Certain religious practices have special meaning for us. We find particular images of God especially comfortable or inspiring. Some saints, because of their lives and deeds, may profoundly appeal to us. Some prayers seem to speak specifically for us, just as some hymns seem to have been composed at our request.

The Catholic faith has an overflowing treasury filled with almost everything ranking from gems to junk! We have an abundance of religious traditions involving sacramentals and saints and images of God, prayers and novenas and other practices. As presiders we need to evaluate carefully the practices of our private lives; we need to assess their value in our development as members of our faith community. We need to ask ourselves, "Where does this practice lead me?"

We are encouraged in our devotions and practices that point us toward God, help us understand the gospel message, assist us in our relationships with our sisters and brothers, and help us bring about the reign of God. We need to be comfortable with a variety of images for God and hold in balance the immanent and transcendent manifestations of the divine. Our prayer lives should reflect God's radical love for us, emphasize relationships rather than individual acts, build community and encourage the development of our gifts. Even the private piety of those who have public roles in the Church must harmonize with the liturgical renewal and reflect the theology of the Second Vatican Council. In this way we strengthen the greater Church, the People of God.

We must be wary of devotions that reflect private religion rather than communal faith and that focus on the devotion itself rather than leading to God. Devotions that contain elements that seem magical, reflect superstitious practices and "guarantee" results based on the practice should be avoided. Devotions that emphasize faith in the saint or the practice rather than faith in God and devotions that serve the agenda of the promoter rather than God's agenda are discouraged. Private devotions should never detract from the Church's public liturgies or emphasize religiosity or piestic behavior or promote superstitious belief

CONSIDER

What are some examples of religious superstition? What are some ways in which private devotion can detract from liturgy?

Have you ever been "turned off" by someone's religious practices? What were they? What was the reason for your response?

How might a presider abuse the privilege of serving the community when presiding?

What responsibilities does a presider have to the assembly? To the individuals served? To the liturgy? To the faith community? To the greater Church?

Popular devotions of the Christian people are to be highly endorsed, provided they accord with the laws and norms of the Church.... But these devotions should be so fashioned that they harmonize with the liturgical seasons, accord with the sacred liturgy, are in some way derived from it, and lead the people to it, since, in fact, the liturgy, by its very nature far surpasses any of them. (Constitution on the Sacred Liturgy, #13)

PRAYER
PREPARATION
PRACTICE
PRAYER

in articles such as statues or medals.

What does all this have to do with our role as presiders? There are three aspects of these devotions we need to consider. Our presiding always reflects our beliefs and practices. Even when each word, gesture and ritual is spelled out for us in a rite book, how we read and pray and enact those ceremonies are all influenced by our personal beliefs and practices. Second, when we preside we are viewed as a representative of the faith community. Presiding is not to be regarded as an opportunity to promote our own personal religious preferences. Finally, there are times when we are free to choose words, prayers and rituals. In these instances, as a representative of the faith community, we must choose those that spread the gospel message and convey God's radical and inclusive love.

Multicultural Liturgies

During the times of the great Catholic immigrations to the United States, the challenge of multicultural faith communities was handled expediently: Each culture built its own church. While the Mass was in Latin at each parish, the language of the sermon was determined by the congregation. At one church it was in German; across the street, Italian; two blocks down, Polish; around the corner, English with a brogue. These peoples instinctively sought out in their faith community what was authentic to them. In many towns and cities, the surplus of church complexes that resulted from such a practice still remains.

Today we view community and liturgy differently. Liturgy celebrates the unity of our diverse beliefs and backgrounds rather than the uniformity of a particular background. Liturgy celebrates not our conformity of culture but our diversity within a universal faith.

The Second Vatican Council renewed the commitment to liturgical adaptation in the areas of language and culture. When we speak of liturgical inculturation we are referrring to the blending of rites and text into the local culture. But what happens when there is more than one "local culture"? While no one should feel like a second-class citizen in his or her own faith community, barriers of language and diversity of customs created by multicultural, multilingual communities present all of us with a challenge.

How do we, as members of the faith community, meet this challenge? How do we, as presiders, respond to the needs of the assembly, especially if we do not speak more than one of the neighborhood languages?

In our role as minister of hospitality, we need to be aware of the diversity within our faith community. As lay presiders who are members of the faith community, we bring a special knowledge and awareness of this assembly to our presiding. While each faith community is unique, here are some general suggestions for meeting these challenges.

Respect diversity. How boring life would be if we were all alike. Diversity presents all of us with opportunities to learn and grow. Focus on what unites, not what divides. We are all children of the one God; we are all related. Use collaborative methods of planning multicultural liturgies. Misunderstanding is likely if the dominant group tries to do something *for* another group instead of *with* them. Mutuality is the goal. Stress that unity with diversity is possible. Strive for real liturgical

CONSIDER

What are the various ethnic and cultural influences in your own life? Irish or Polish or Hispanic Catholic? British Anglican? African Methodist Episcopalian? German or Scandinavian Lutheran? Native American spirituality? South or Central American Catholic? New England transcendentalism? Japanese Shintoism? Other?

How did these elements influence your Catholicism?

What factors influence your faith today?

What are the various cultural influences in your faith community? How are they expressed?

Are there people in your faith community who feel like second-class citizens because of differences in language and cultural background? Are they able to worship authentically within your community? If not, what can be done to improve the situation?

What are some ways in which the community can become more hospitable?

Even in the liturgy, the Church has no wish to impose a rigid uniformity in matters that do not affect the faith or the good of the whole community; rather the Church respects and fosters the genius and talents of the various races and peoples. The Church studies with sympathy and, if possible, preserves intact the elements in these peoples' way of life that are not indissolubly bound up with superstition and error. Sometimes in fact the Church admits these elements into the liturgy itself, provided they are in keeping with the true and authentic spirit of the liturgy. (Constitution on the Sacred Liturgy, #37)

presence of the minority group(s), not tokenism. Emphasize mutual respect. Recognize that we gather for one another, no matter what our differences. Be aware of similar efforts in neighboring communities in order to pool opportunities and talents.

We all belong to the greater Church. Insist that all groups and individuals refrain from stereotyping others. Create a supportive environment for dialogue. Recognize that these identical problems have been present within the Church from its beginning. Provide opportunities for education: workshops in the cultural histories; language "crash courses" for musicians; introduction to the art of diverse cultures; ethnic and cultural concerts, recitals, dance programs. Celebrate multilingual liturgies at the high points of the liturgical year. Let art and the liturgical environment recognize the community's cultures.

Include the music of Taizé and other multilingual music. Celebrate feasts of special significance to the several cultures. Be open to creative ways of doing ritual. Perhaps a funeral vigil may be conducted in one language and the funeral itself in another. Or pastoral caregivers who speak different languages may alternate their visits to a local nursing home. Maintain cross-cultural dialogue within the community. Refer to the *Guidelines for Multilingual Masses* (Bishops' Committee on the Liturgy, available from the United States Catholic Conference) and other available resources.

One caution should be noted. While we want to recognize the ethnic backgrounds of the members of the assembly, we use these symbols and rituals with great care. As pointed out in the section on symbols, the rituals and traditions of a culture usually have a variety of meanings. In addition, they may be considered proper or fitting only in specific times or places. We who are not of that tradition need to be mindful of our use of such symbols and rituals, always treating them with reverence.

▶ *"When I was a young girl a friend, who was not Catholic, saw my rosary on the dresser. 'What a pretty cross and necklace,' she said, picking it up and putting it around her neck. I was incensed at her sacrilege! Now, remembering that scene so vividly, I am very careful about picking up objects or rituals from another faith tradition, lest I too perform what someone else might consider to be a sacrilege."*

Liturgies With Special Groups

The concept of community means that we gather in our diversity; through ritual, prayer and belief, we become one. That is our larger faith community; that is the group with which we gather for Sunday worship.

However, many of us often choose to gather also with those with whom we have something in common. This mutual element may be vocation, age, gender, place of employment or schooling, interest, location, sexual orientation, relationship. We pray with our faith-sharing group, the alumni association, the sports team, the befrienders' group, the women's organization, the Christian Initiation team and others. We pray together in recognition of what we have in common and to strengthen this already existing bond.

This smaller group is our community within a community. In these groups we gather, we use symbols, we have music, we create sacred

CONSIDER

When have you experienced an especially meaningful special liturgy? What made it so memorable?

What can you do, as a member of the assembly, to make your Sunday liturgies more Spirit-filled and prayerful?

What can you do, as a presider, to help the assembly celebrate a liturgy that is filled with spiritual meaning?

Often the problem of diversity can be mitigated by supplementing the parish Sunday celebration with special celebrations for smaller homogeneous groups.... Nevertheless, it would be out of harmony with the Lord's wish for unity in his Church if believers were to worship only in such homogeneous groupings (AP). (Music in Catholic Worship, #18)

CONSIDER

What are some of the significant milestones of life that our society does not recognize? Why do you think they are not celebrated?

When have you experienced an event that you wanted to ritualize with others but were unable to do so? Why did you want to recognize it? Why were you hesitant or unable to do so?

Today, what would you choose to ritualize in your life? What would you like to ritualize for those close to you? Why don't you?

space, we have prayer and ritual, we have liturgy. In these groups we especially experience the collaboration called for in the Second Vatican Council: mutual collaboration, shared leadership and presiding, interdependence, an absence of elitism and control, an equality yet diversity of ministry, solidarity and bonding, a firm commitment to hospitality.

These celebrations of select groups help us develop our prayer life; they contribute to the foundation stones we bring to our larger and more diverse community liturgies. While these prayer experiences may feed our soul, they do not fulfill our need for the greater community. It is only in that diversity that we can respond fully to the gospel challenge presented to us by God's radical and inclusive love.

Rites and Blessings for Everyday Life

As we baptized Christians claim our heritage as people of prayer, we find ourselves bringing prayer and ritual outside the church building and into our everyday life. The vision of the Second Vatican Council leads us to recognize our own sacredness, the sanctity of our everyday life, the sanctity of the world. This is not the imposition of religion and ritual upon our existence; it is the recognition of the sacredness that already exists everywhere.

We want and need prayer and ritual; we seek prayer and ritual to honor the significant occasions of our lives, to help us through the difficult times, to accompany us through life's passages, to celebrate the joyous times, to unite us into community. Our tradition has long ritualized many significant occasions of life. Many beautiful blessing prayers within the treasury of the Church are rarely prayed because people are unaware of them or believe they are reserved to the ordained.

In informal groups of friends, family and neighbors, we continue the tradition of prayer and ritual and seek ways to ritualize many more events and circumstances: retirement; planting a garden; engagements and wedding anniversaries; the return of a family member; healing following a divorce or separation; entering the military; bringing home an adopted child; Mother's Day; Father's Day; beginning or ending a school year; honoring a friend; the acquisition of a new work of art; being accepted into the seminary or convent; the changes of the seasons; redecorating a room; leaving on or returning from vacation; birthdays; a first menstrual period; the completion of a college degree; a new house; the acquisition of farm animals; planting a tree; the healing of a woman who has had an abortion; a retiree entering the Peace Corps; harvest time; moving into a senior community or nursing home; a blessing before surgery; a new pet; getting a driver's license; pregnancy; a return to health and wholeness; the first anniversary of widowhood; selling the family home; a new job or promotion; the overcoming of a barrier for handicapped people, minorities or women; the attainment of a long-sought goal; the completion of chemotherapy or radiation treatments....

All these—and more—are worthy of celebrating and ritualizing. Scripture, tradition and psalmody give us the building blocks with which to construct these celebrations. We include music and ritual; we use environment, symbols and art to create sacred space; we gather, forming community; in other words, we have liturgy.

> ▶ *"We gathered to celebrate my becoming a mother-in-law. The gifts that my friends presented to me were their inspiring and humorous and poignant mother-in-law stories. And then each blessed me with words of wisdom and prayers of love. What a wonderful way to be launched into this so often maligned role!"*

Commissioning of a Lay Presider

A parish's formal response to lay presiders (or lay preachers) can take many forms. Some of us lay presiders have what might be called a battlefield commission. We happened to be handy when an emergency arose and, in answer to both the emergency and the promptings of the Holy Spirit, we responded with our own yes. We accepted the role of lay presider as a natural extension of our baptismal right and responsibility.

In other instances, a faith community may go through a formal process to choose potential lay presiders, give them specific training and provide opportunities for learning. Then at the completion of the program the person is declared ready to preside.

In either instance a community may decide to have a formal commissioning of lay presiders (or lay preachers). This confers upon the lay presider the ritualized blessing of the assembly and the support of the faith community and affirms the ministry of the lay presider.

CONSIDER

What is the tradition in your parish regarding lay presiders? What are the strengths of that tradition? The weaknesses?

What does a formal commissioning say about a faith community and lay presiders?

How do you feel about being commissioned at a Sunday liturgy? Why?

In the life of a parish there is a diversity of services that are exercised by lay persons. It is fitting that as people publicly begin their service they receive the blessing of God who gives the gifts needed to carry out this work. (Book of Blessings, #1808)

The New Presider

All learning endeavors conclude with inevitable closing comments, last-minute reminders and summaries, along with good wishes and benedictions. So, too, this handbook closes with the familiar declaration that what is now nearly concluded is but a beginning.

> *Divine and Eternal Spirit,*
> *you call us as your people,*
> *to gather and pray.*
> *You lead us as pilgrims;*
> *you bless us with a vision of Church—*
> *a vision of what we are all called to be.*
> *Empower us!*
> *Empower us to empower others*
> *to pray,*
> *to minister,*
> *to be vulnerable,*
> *to be receptive to your transforming fire.*
> *Direct us all*
> *that what we now do*
> *may help bring forth your reign.*
> *We ask this in hope-filled humility and fearful awe,*
> *for you, with Christ and the Creator,*
> *are the Indivisible God Most High,*
> *who lives forever and ever. Amen.*

CONSIDER

What are the most difficult things for you to remember when you are presiding? Why?

Could you describe to someone the flow of the liturgy for which you are presiding? Do you have a sense of the entire liturgy?

What can you do to get a better sense of the liturgy? How can you learn to remember all the necessary details?

Details

As we have said from the first, good, effective presiding requires attention to details. At first the details seem overwhelming, but gradually, as we observe, prepare, practice and preside, comes the recognition that all these details fall into three main categories: (1) general presiding rules and guidelines; (2) the rites of each type of liturgy; (3) the details of this specific liturgy.

With experience, the details of presiding gradually become less intimidating. We begin to feel at ease with posture and gesture, with vesture and worship space, with praying aloud and doing ritual. They begin to feel more natural to us.

The details of each type of liturgy also become more familiar with repetition. The more often we preside at Morning or Evening Prayer, the deeper grows our understanding of it. The same holds true for the other liturgies.

The details of this specific liturgy, however, will always have to be dealt with separately. There will always be details to be remembered: movement and ritual particulars for this worship space; the music for this liturgy; time constraints, if necessary; people's names at funerals or funeral vigils; the current idiosyncrasy of the sound system; announcements to be made and so on.

However, the more we preside, the easier it is for us to enter into public prayer. Presiding is praying!

▶ *"I was so angry at the presider at my uncle's funeral! My aunt and uncle had belonged to that parish for over fifty years and had been active in that faith community until the last few years when my uncle's illness dominated both their lives. At the funeral the presider referred to my aunt by two different names—both wrong! I sat there praying that she wasn't listening!"*

A Common Error

In some faith communities the presider will be handed a completed text of a rite; the individual will be expected to prepare and practice that rite, but need not be concerned further about the music or environment or rituals. In other communities the presider may have to write or choose each and every word and ritual. Being too wordy is an error commonly committed in this latter situation.

We need to remember that a surplus of words cheapens the totality of those words. When it comes to the number of words in a liturgy often less is more.

The liturgy—the work of the people—should include music, ritual and silence. The assembly should be involved. Verbal communication needs to be balanced by symbolic activity; the liturgy should not be filled with readings and preaching and prayers and explanations of rituals and symbols. In our planning it is helpful to remember that most of us talk better than we listen!

We need to let the rituals and symbols speak for themselves. We must not be afraid to model the ritual and let the assembly follow our example. We must not be afraid of silence. The Holy Spirit is present and far surpasses us at transforming minds and hearts.

Improving Our Presiding

When we begin this new ministry it is helpful if we preside several times in close succession. If too much time elapses between presiding opportunities, it becomes difficult to profit from the experience, for each time becomes another first. To improve upon previous experience we need to be able to recall the earlier service, how it went, how we felt, what we would do differently, how we might prepare better.

Feedback about our presiding can also be most helpful. Evaluations from the other liturgical ministers and from the assembly let us know about our effectiveness and alert us to areas that need improvement. Again, having a liturgy committee or a support group that meets to discuss liturgy can be invaluable. In this community within the larger community all critiquing should be done considerately and sensitively. Establishing a tradition that each person offer more positive comments than negative helps maintain a constructive atmosphere.

Opening and closing the meetings with prayer reminds us of what we, as liturgical ministers, are to be doing with and for our faith community. The prayers in this book can be used by individuals or

CONSIDER

How comfortable are you in planning a liturgy or ritual? Why? What kind of background or experience do you need to do a better job of liturgy planning? Where can you get this knowledge, experience or help?

When have you attended a liturgy that was too wordy? What was your reaction? What would have improved the service? How can you avoid planning a liturgy that is too wordy?

What special experience and background do you bring to liturgy planning? To presiding?

CONSIDER

What support is available to new presiders in your community?

What kind of honest and constructive feedback is available when you begin presiding? How helpful is the response from the community or other liturgical ministers?

What place does prayer have in your liturgy meetings?

What can you do to be supportive of other new presiders?

groups. The following prayer, which was used before the meetings of the Second Vatican Council, can also serve as a model for how to approach our work of liturgy and of bringing forth the reign of God.

> We are here before you, O Holy Spirit,
> conscious of our innumerable sins,
> but united in a special way in your holy name.
> Come and abide with us.
> Deign to penetrate our hearts.
> Be the guide of our actions,
> indicate the path we should take,
> and show us what we must do
> so that, with your help,
> our work may be in all things pleasing to you.
> May you be our only inspiration
> and the overseer of our intentions,
> for you alone possess a glorious name
> together with the Father and the Son.
> May you, who are infinite justice,
> never permit that we be disturbers of justice.
> Let not our ignorance induce us to evil,
> nor flattery sway us,
> nor moral and material interest corrupt us.
> But unite our hearts to you alone,
> and do it strongly, so that,
> with the gift of your grace,
> we may be one in you
> and may in nothing depart from the truth.
> Thus, united in your name,
> may we in our every action
> follow the dictates of your mercy and justice,
> so that today and always
> our judgments may not be alien to you
> and in eternity we may obtain
> the unending reward of our actions. Amen.

▶ *"I attended a week-long lay presiding workshop at a Catholic university. We practiced in small groups, were videotaped in our presiding, and were critiqued by the instructor. After my turn at presiding the instructor, abiding by the rule he had imposed, began with the positive comments. Moving to the negative, he said, 'You added a word.' 'I what?' 'When you read that prayer you concluded it with "And we ask this through Christ our Lord." There's no and written in the text.' I hope I responded graciously to this criticism, although a bit incredulously. Knowing the type of presiding I would be expected to do in my community, adding one word to a prayer was not my main concern."*

Continuing on...

The call to preside is never simply a commitment to be at a certain place to carry out presiding duties. By our response to that call we enter into a

PRAYER
PR**E**PARATION
PR**A**CTICE
PRA**Y**ER

CONSIDER

What means are available to you for continuing to learn about liturgy and presiding? How practical is this?

How do you intend to continue to grow in your prayer life?

How can you maintain your interest in presiding and in liturgy?

How will you sustain your sense of awe and wonder?

How can you remain reverent?

What is the basis for your hospitality?

Who and what do you love?

covenant between ourself and God's assembly. Our duties in that covenant include: our sincere best efforts in prayer, both private and public; hospitality and reverence in our presiding; an openness to serve both the liturgy and the assembly; a commitment to prepare and to practice for the liturgies; preserving a sense of awe; a willingness to be transformed by the Spirit, by the liturgy and by presiding; maintaining our passionate love of God, ourself, community, liturgy; an ongoing relationship with God; a commitment to be ever growing and studying in our presiding ministry.

Becoming a presider means accepting a responsibility to continue to develop. Fortunately, this is an exciting time in Church history with an abundance of resources available.

Our faith community, through the assembly, parish staff and larger Church community, offers opportunities in faith and presider development. Nearly every diocese has an office to help people who are involved in liturgical ministry. This office may be called a worship center, worship office, liturgy office, office of liturgy and spirituality or something similar. Most of these centers provide updated information about liturgy, including lay presiding, conduct workshops on issues of current interest and serve as resource centers.

A rapidly growing collection of useful materials is available, including books, newsletters, periodicals, audio tapes, videos and various ministry aids (see Resources, pages 135-145).

Most Catholic colleges, universities and seminaries have classes, seminars, workshops, conferences and lectures that are open to interested people. And, in this ecumenical age, many non-Catholic seminaries also have good Catholic resources. Various local and national liturgical organizations offer classes and workshops around the country. With the tremendous variety of new materials becoming available to us, we have only to recognize our needs and begin the process.

Familiarity with the documents of Vatican II is most helpful in establishing a foundation in liturgy. Especially important are:

- *Constitution on the Church*
- *Constitution on the Sacred Liturgy*
- *Constitution on the Church in the Modern World*
- *Decree on the Apostolate of the Laity*
- *Declaration on Religious Freedom*
- *Declaration on the Relationship of the Church to Non-Christians*
- *Closing Messages of the Council*

We also need to be familiar with the liturgical publications of the National Conference of Catholic Bishops, especially:

- Music in Catholic Worship
- Environment and Art in Catholic Worship
- Liturgy of the Hours

The rites books themselves, especially the introductions, offer much information for the new presider. And, they are worth reviewing occasionally even for the experienced presider (see Resources, pages 135-136, for a complete listing).

There are many fine periodicals dealing with liturgy, Scripture, worship, prayer, liturgical ministries, preaching, music, dance, environment, Church history, spirituality. Since the parish or staff may subscribe to some of these publications setting up a lending library would make them accessible to presiders and other liturgical ministers of the faith community. The parish may also subscribe for the ministers, or the ministers themselves may find it helpful to have their own subscriptions.

▶ *"I can't imagine a responsible physician or lawyer not continuing to read and study and learn. As a lay presider, I consider myself a professional in the best sense of the term. I too have a duty to continue to grow within the ministry."*

One Last Note

The Second Vatican Council has given us a new vision: a vision drawing us away from our institutional images of Church to inspire us to build Church as community; a vision moving us from a rigid uniformity in liturgy to a recognition of the importance of culture in liturgy; a vision authenticating liturgy as the work of the assembly; a vision challenging a dogmatic approach to faith and offering in its place an atmosphere of open questioning; a vision verifying the talents and charisms and personal faith experiences of laypeople as gifts given to the entire Church; a vision continuing to inspire and empower.

We celebrate the vibrancy of the Council and in the courageous tradition of those gathered, continue to venture forward on the Spirit-led path that they began. We are the Body of Christ in the world today—let us help bring forth the reign of God!

Resources

Anew presider or a person interested in liturgy will find that available resources cover the entire spectrum from introductory to scholarly. In response to great interest in the theology of worship, creative liturgies, Morning and Evening Prayer, and the expanded role of lay ministry, many book publishers are expanding their product lines to include multilingual publications, materials suitable for children and youth and the aged, aids for lay pastoral caregivers, and audiovisual materials and software relevant to many different ministries. Some of these publishers also sponsor stimulating and informative workshops, lectures, conferences, conventions.

Check your local area for liturgical or ministry associations and local branches of national organizations. Catholic (and non-Catholic) colleges and universities and seminaries (including library facilities) are valuable sources of help. The diocesan liturgy center, liturgy office or worship center is a good contact place for courses and workshops and conferences as well as publications.

The following list should be considered as a starting point, directing the reader to other materials of interest, instruction or inspiration. Catalogues are available by calling or writing the publishers or organizations.

Rite Books

Order of Christian Funerals. Prepared by International Commission on English in the Liturgy, A Joint Commission of Catholic Bishops' Conferences. Chicago: Liturgy Training Publications, 1989.

The Rites of the Catholic Church as revised by the Second Vatican Ecumenical Council. Volume I, Initiation. Prepared by the International Commission on English in the Liturgy, A Joint Commission of Catholic Bishops' Conferences. New York: Pueblo Publishing Company, Inc., 1988.

The Rites of the Catholic Church as revised by Decree of the Second Vatican Ecumenical Council, and published by Authority of Pope Paul VI. Prepared by the International Commission on English in the Liturgy, Volume Two. New York: Pueblo Publishing Company, Inc., 1980.

Book of Blessings. Prepared by International Commission on English in the Liturgy, A Joint Commission of Catholic Bishops' Conferences. Collegeville, Minn.: The Liturgical Press, 1989.

Catholic Household Blessings & Prayers. Bishops' Committee on the Liturgy, National Conference of Catholic Bishops. Washington, D.C.: The United States Catholic Conference, Inc., 1988.

Sunday Celebrations in the Absence of a Priest. Prepared by the Committee on the Liturgy, National Conference of Catholic Bishops. New York: Catholic Book Publishing Co., 1994.

A Ritual for Laypersons: Rites for Holy Communion and the Pastoral Care of the Sick and Dying. Collegeville, Minn.: The Liturgical Press, 1993.

Liturgical Publishers

These publishing houses offer a great variety of helps for liturgical ministers.

Celebration Publications provides much practical assistance for those in ministry. They offer the following periodicals: *Eucharistic Minister; The Caring Community; Christian Initiation; Lector; Celebration,* an ecumenical worship resource magazine.

> Celebration Publications
> P.O. Box 419493
> Kansas City, MO 64141-6493
> Telephone: 800-333-7373

The Liturgical Press specializes in materials dealing with liturgy. Their comprehensive output runs the gamut from introductory and contemporary to historical and academic; it also includes Pueblo Books, Michael Glazier Books and *Worship,* a scholarly journal.

> The Liturgical Press
> St. John's Abbey
> P.O. Box 7500
> Collegeville, MN 56321-7500
> Telephone: 800-858-5450
> Fax: 800-445-5899

Liturgy Training Publications (LTP), in faithfulness to its name, is an excellent source of practical materials for the Church's liturgy. Accompanying its significant book and pamphlet output are the following periodicals: *Liturgy 90; Environment & Art Letter: A Forum on Architecture and the Arts for the Parish; Plenty Good Room,* which focuses on the African American worship experience in the Catholic Church.

> Liturgy Training Publications (LTP)
> 1800 North Hermitage Avenue
> Chicago, IL 60622-1101
> Telephone: 800-933-1800
> Fax: 800-933-7094

The National Association of Pastoral Musicians (NPM) is an organization for those involved in liturgical and pastoral ministry—not just musicians. It publishes *Pastoral Music* magazine, books and tapes, as well as sponsoring numerous conferences, workshops and conventions of value to people at almost every level of involvement and expertise.

> National Association of Pastoral Musicians
> 225 Sheridan Street, N.W.
> Washington, DC 20011
> Telephone: 202-723-5800
> Fax: 202-723-2262

NPM's books, music, and videotapes are available from The Pastoral Press.

> The Pastoral Press
> P.O. Box 1470
> Laurel, MD 20725
> Telephone: 800-976-9669
> Fax: 800-979-9669

The Notre Dame Center for Pastoral Liturgy is dedicated to continuing the liturgical renewal through providing resources and personnel for educational programs, conferences and workshops, and through publishing books, videos, and the periodicals *Liturgy Digest* and *Assembly*.

> Notre Dame Center for Pastoral Liturgy
> P.O. Box 81
> Notre Dame, IN 46556
> Telephone: 219-631-5435
> Fax: 219-631-6968

Resource Publications publishes *Modern Liturgy*, a magazine devoted to assisting liturgical ministers, in addition to a wide array of supportive materials.

> Resource Publications, Inc.
> 160 East Virginia Street, #290
> San Jose, CA 95112
> Telephone: 800-736-7600
> Fax: 408-287-8748

Music Publishers

While the following publishers specialize in music, they also have additional materials for presiders and pastoral caregivers.

American Catholic Press
16565 South State Street
South Holland, IL 60473
Telephone: 708-331-5485

GIA Publications, Inc.
7404 South Mason Avenue
Chicago, IL 60638
Telephone: 800-442-1358
Fax: 708-496-3828

Oregon Catholic Press (OCP)
5536 N.E. Hassalo
Portland, OR 97213
Telephone: 800-548-8749
Fax: 800-843-8181

Trinity Music, Inc.
P.O. Box 1470
Laurel, MD 20725
Telephone: 800-976-9669
Fax: 800-979-9669

World Library Publications, Inc.
3815 North Willow Road
P.O. Box 2701
Schiller Park, IL 60176-0701
Telephone: 800-566-6150
Fax: 708-671-5715

General Publishers

Many publishers offer materials in the areas of personal prayer, Bible study, theology, children's programs, the catechumenate, Church history, inspiration, adult education, devotions. The following is a list of publishers whose catalogues also include materials in the areas of liturgy, ritual or presiding.

Abingdon Press
201 Eighth Avenue South
Nashville, TN 37203
Telephone: 615-749-6290
Fax: 615-749-6512

Augsburg Fortress Publishers
426 South Fifth Street
Box 1209
Minneapolis, MN 55440
Telephone: 612-330-3300

Ave Maria Press
Notre Dame, IN 46556
Telephone: 219-287-2831
              800-282-1865

Concordia Publishing House
3558 South Jefferson Avenue
St. Louis, MO 63118
Telephone: 314-268-1000

The Crossroad Publishing Company
370 Lexington Avenue
New York, NY 10017
Telephone: 212-532-3650

Forest of Peace Books, Inc.
Route One, Box 248
Topeka, KS 66608

Harper Collins Publishers, Inc.
10 East 53rd Street
New York, NY 10022
Telephone: 212-207-7000

Harper San Francisco
1160 Battery Street
San Francisco, CA 94111
Telephone: 415-477-4400

Orbis Books
P.O. Box 308
Maryknoll, NY 10545-0308
Telephone: 800-258-5838

Paulist Press
997 Macarthur Boulevard
Mahwah, NJ 07430
Telephone: 201-825-7300
Fax: 201-825-8345

Resurrection Press Ltd.
P.O. Box 248
Williston Park, NY 11596-0248
Telephone: 800-892-6657
Fax: 516-746-6872

St. Anthony Messenger Press
1615 Republic Street
Cincinnati, OH 45210-1298
Telephone: 800-488-0488
Fax: 513-241-1197

Sheed & Ward
115 East Armour Boulevard
P.O. Box 419492
Kansas City, MO 64141-6492
Telephone: 800-333-7373

Source Books
Box 794
Trabuco Canyon, CA 92678

Tabor Publishing
(Includes Thomas More & Christian Classics)
P.O. Box 7000
Allen, TX 75002-1305
Telephone: 800-822-6701
Fax: 800-688-8356

Twenty-Third Publications
185 Willow Street
P.O. Box 180
Mystic, CT 06355
Telephone: 800-321-0411
Fax: 203-572-0788

Organizations

These organizations and associations deal with various types of ministry.

The BeFriender Ministry is a national Christian program to empower laypeople in the pastoral care of others. It provides regional training workshops and continuing support and education.

BeFriender Ministry
University of St. Thomas
Mail #SOD
2260 Summit Avenue
St. Paul, MN 55105-1094
Telephone: 612-962-5775

The National Association of Pastoral Musicians (NPM) is an organization for those involved in liturgical and pastoral ministry—not just musicians. It sponsors numerous conferences, workshops and conventions of value to people at almost every level of involvement and expertise.

> National Association of Pastoral Musicians
> 225 Sheridan Street, N.W.
> Washington, DC 20011
> Telephone: 202-723-5800
> Fax: 202-723-2262

The National Pastoral Life Center is dedicated to supporting pastoral ministry and parish life. In addition to publishing books, pamphlets and videos, it also sponsors conventions and publishes the quarterly magazine *Church*.

> National Pastoral Life Center
> 299 Elizabeth Street
> New York, NY 10012-2806
> Telephone: 212-431-7825
> Fax: 212-274-9786

The Stephen Ministries is an ecumenical program that trains people to become "Stephen Leaders," who in turn train people in their own parishes to provide one-to-one care to those in need.

> Stephen Ministries
> 8016 Dale
> St. Louis, MO 63117-1449
> Telephone: 314-645-5511

Selected Specific Resources

Here is a list of books and tapes that offer insight, theological and historical background, support and practical suggestions in various areas of ministry.

Leonardo Boff's *Sacraments of Life: Life of the Sacraments* looks at how sacraments and symbols and stories reveal God's presence in everyday life. This excellent small volume is published by The Pastoral Press, 1987.

The instructional video *Leading the Community in Prayer—The Art of Presiding for Deacons and Lay Persons*, by John Brooks-Leonard (The Liturgical Press), concentrates on the visual elements of presiding and offers much for the beginning presider as well as those with experience.

Joseph Campbell's book and video series *The Power of Myth*, with Bill Moyers, is a fascinating study of humanity's long and intimate involvement with story and ritual. The book was published by Doubleday (1540 Broadway, New York, NY 10036; telephone: 212-354-6500, fax: 212-202-7985) in 1988, and the video set by Mystic Fire Video (P.O. Box 30969, Dept. DL, New York, NY 10011; telephone: 800-727-8433).

Religious Signing: The New Comprehensive Guide for all Faiths by Elaine Costello (Bantam Books, 1540 Broadway, New York, NY 10036; telephone: 212-354-6500, fax: 212-202-7985), published in 1986, contains the signs for words and phrases that may not be included in other signing books.

Melva Wilson Costen, in *African American Christian Worship* (Abingdon Press, 1993), documents that heritage as embodied in its music and rituals and ordinances.

Christ is Coming: Celebrating Advent, Christmas & Epiphany (St. Anthony Messenger Press, 1992), and *Christ is Risen: Celebrating Lent, Easter & Pentecost* (St. Anthony Messenger Press, 1994), by Theresa Cotter, contain daily meditations, prayers, rituals and projects for the liturgical seasons.

The Dilemma of Priestless Sundays by James Dallen (Liturgy Training Publications, 1994) looks at this impending crisis and presents alternative ways of dealing with it.

Frontiers of Hispanic Theology in the United States, edited by Allan Figueroa Deck, S.J. (Orbis Books, 1992), is a collection of writings presenting various Catholic perspectives within the Hispanic culture.

Lucien Deiss and Gloria Weyman collaborated on *Dance for the Lord* (World Library Publications, 1975), a well-illustrated book with corresponding audiocassette. This book may be out of print, but a diocesan liturgy office may have it in its resource center.

PeaceRites by Carla Desola (The Pastoral Press, 1993) is a series of workshops combining prayer, Scripture, movement and music in a nonthreatening, noncompetitive environment for nondancers.

The Disabled God: Toward a Liberatory Theology of Disability by Nancy L. Eiesland (Abingdon Press, 1994), challenges current attitudes, practice and images of people labeled as "handicapped."

Mem Fox and Julie Vivas's *Wilfrid Gordon McDonald Partridge* (Kane/Miller Book Publishers, P.O. Box 529, Brooklyn, NY 11231) is a delightful picture book for all ages.

In his entertaining and nontechnical style, Robert Fulghum discusses the basic human need to celebrate (ritualize) the significant events of human existence in his book *From Beginning to End: The Rituals of Our Lives* (New York: Ballantine Books, 1995).

Introducing Dance in Christian Worship, by Ronald Gagne, Thomas Kane and Robert VerEecke (The Pastoral Press, 1984) contains a history of liturgical dance and many suggestions for incorporating dance as sacred art in the "here and now."

Edwina Gateley challenges complacency, sanctimoniousness and un-demonstrated faith in her audiotapes and books, which include the book *A Warm Moist Salty God: Women Journeying Towards Wisdom*, (Source Books, 1993), and the audiocassette *Discipleship: Turning the World Upside Down* (St. Anthony Messenger Press, 1991).

Edward Hays proclaims the sacredness of all of life in his creative prayers, such as those in *Prayers for a Planetary Pilgrim* (Forest of Peace, 1988) and *Prayers for the Domestic Church: A Handbook for Worship in the Home* (Forest of Peace, 1989).

Monika K. Hellwig's fine little book *The Eucharist and the Hunger of the World* (Sheed & Ward, 1992) looks at the many meanings of hunger and the mystery of Eucharist—not as a thing but as an action.

Robert Hovda was a wise and prophetic voice in the liturgical renewal movement. The Liturgical Press continues to publish his book *Strong, Loving and Wise—Presiding in Liturgy* (1983) and also *The "Amen Corner"* (1994) a collection of Hovda's columns from *Worship* magazine, edited by John F. Baldovin, S.J.

Gabe Huck's editing of *A Sourcebook about Liturgy* (Liturgy Training Publications, 1994) brings together some truly wonderful words about liturgy.

Bill Huebsch is a continuing passionate voice for Vatican II and its reforms, as evidenced in *Rethinking Sacraments—Holy Moments in Daily Living* (Twenty-Third Publications, 1989), and *Vatican II in Plain English* (Thomas More Press, Tabor Publishing, 1996).

Aidan Kavanagh's collection of wisdom is entitled *Elements of Rite: A Handbook of Liturgical Style* (Pueblo Publishing Co., The Liturgical Press, 1982). Kavanagh's terse comments are still pertinent and needed.

Catherine H. Krier has compiled a primer for environmental planning based on the lectionary in *Symbols for all Seasons: Environmental Planning for Cycles A, B & C* (Resource Publications, Inc., 1988).

Madeleine L'Engle's *The Irrational Season* (HarperSanFrancisco, 1983) is a beautifully personal, poetically inspirational look at the liturgical year.

Peter Mazar, in his book *To Crown the Year: Decorating the Church Through the Seasons* (Liturgy Training Publications, 1994), offers practical suggestions for creating prayerful environments for worship.

Richard P. McBrien, in his wonderfully readable *Ministry, A Theological, Pastoral Handbook* (HarperSanFrancisco, 1988) presents a history of ministry, including its meaning and mystery and spirituality.

Rosemary Catalano Mitchell and Gail Anderson Ricciuti's *Birthings and Blessings, Liberating Worship Services for the Inclusive Church, volumes I and II* (The Crossroad Publishing Company, 1991) is a wonderful resource for creative and powerful rituals.

Gertrude Mueller Nelson's *To Dance with God* (Paulist Press, 1986) is a collection of practical rituals celebrating the year for family and community.

In Her Own Rite: Constructing Feminist Liturgical Tradition (Abingdon Press, 1990) is Marjorie Procter-Smith's classic and well-written exploration of the liturgical tradition and the feminist movement.

Gail Ramshaw and Judy Jarrett's *Sunday Morning* (Liturgy Training Publications, 1993) presents liturgy in pictures and terms that children can enjoy and understand. Would that all those who gather had this level of comprehension!

Klemens Richter presents another discussion of symbols and rituals and gestures in *The Meaning of the Sacramental Symbols: Answers to Today's Questions* (The Liturgical Press, 1990).

Earth Prayers from Around the World: 365 Prayers, Poems, and Invocations for Honoring the Earth, edited by Elizabeth Robers and Elias Amidon (HarperSanFrancisco, 1991), testifies eloquently to how much all of humanity has in common.

Our Lady of Guadalupe: Faith and Empowerment Among Mexican-American Women, by Jeanette Rodriguez (University of Texas Press, Box 7819, Austin, TX 78713-7819, 1994), is the result of a study of the Guadalupe event, a powerful religious symbol that goes beyond devotionalism.

Joyce Rupp, O.S.M., in *Praying Our Goodbyes* (Ave Maria Press, 1988), has collected prayers offering reassurance that the pain and loss of goodbye need not destroy but can enrich the life journey.

Sandy Eisenberg Sasso's ecumenical picture book *In God's Name* (Jewish Lights Publishing, P.O. Box 237, Sunset Farm Office, Rt. 4, Woodstock, VT 05091, 1994) looks at how God is addressed, which is important for everyone, not just children.

Mark Searle's appropriately titled book *Liturgy Made Simple*, first published by The Liturgical Press in 1981, has been reissued. Searle was also editor for the newsletter *Assembly*. The December 1979 issue, "Liturgical Gestures," is an eight-page collection of beautiful meditations; the booklet *Liturgical Gestures, Words, Objects* (1995) is an expansion of the earlier newsletter and was published in honor of Mark Searle and edited by Eleanor Bernstein, C.S.J. Both are published by the Notre Dame Center for Pastoral Liturgy.

Virginia Sloyan edited *A Sourcebook About Christian Death* (Liturgy Training Publications, 1990). This collection of writings about life, death and resurrection offers much to those who mourn, those who preside, those who seek.

Howard Thurman, poet and theologian, considers the meanings of the black spirituals in his books *Deep River* (1975) and *The Negro Spiritual Speaks of Life and Death* (1975), available from Friends United Press, 101 Quaker Hill Drive, Richmond, IN 47374; telephone: 317-962-7573.

Maren C. Tirabassi and Kathy Wonson Eddy in their book *Gifts of Many Cultures: Worship Resources for the Global Community*, 1975 (United Church Press, Cleveland, OH 44115) present a wonderfully diverse collection of prayers, poems, rituals and art from around the world for ecumenical and other services.

Miriam Therese Winter writes as a Catholic religious, a liturgical musician, a worker in global poverty, a seminary professor, a woman. Among her books are *WomanWord* (Crossroad, 1990), *Woman Prayer Woman Song: Resources for Ritual* (Crossroad, 1987), and *Why Sing? Toward a Theology of Catholic Church Music* (The Pastoral Press, 1987).

Douglas Wood and Cheng-Khee Chee's award-winning *Old Turtle* (Pfeifer-Hamilton Publishers, 210 West Michigan, Duluth, MN 55802, 1991) is another beautifully illustrated book for all ages.

Brian Wren's book *What Language Shall I Borrow? God-Talk in Worship: A Male Response to Feminist Theology* (Crossroad, 1990) examines the power of language as understood by a poet-theologian.